A Preacher's

A Preacher's Life of Jesus

George B. Duncan

HODDER AND STOUGHTON

LONDON SYDNEY AUCKLAND TORONTO

British Library Cataloguing in Publication data

Duncan, George Baillie
  A preacher's life of Jesus.
  1. Jesus Christ-Biography-Meditations
  I. Title
  232.9'01   BT301.2

ISBN 0 340 24699 5

First published 1979

Set, printed and bound in Great Britain for
Hodder and Stoughton Limited,
Mill Road, Dunton Green, Sevenoaks, Kent,
by Cox & Wyman Ltd, Reading

Preface

WHEN I WAS asked to write a book to be called *A Preacher's Life of Jesus* I found myself facing two immense problems. The first problem was the sheer impossibility of compressing into one book of sermons the story, or even a fraction of the whole story, of that amazing life which has changed the world. All I could hope to do was to gather together messages dealing with various facets of His life and its meaning for men and women living in our day. That is what I have tried to do, taking incidents, sayings, miracles, and parables that cover the whole span from Bethlehem to Calvary, from His birth to His death and resurrection. It was said of Him while He lived on earth, 'Never man spake like this man.' That of course was true, it was also true that never was man born like this man, never man did what this man did, never man died like this man. If you are looking for a history of His life then you will be disappointed. If on the other hand you are looking for something of the meaning of that birth, life and death for men today, I hope that as you read these pages you will not be disappointed.

The other difficulty I faced is that in many quarters preaching is regarded as out of date. I am however reminded of a saying in *The Trouble with the Church* by Helmut Thielicke: 'Wherever we find a vital living congregation, we find at its centre vital preaching.' I believe this to be true. After a life-time in the ministry in which my task has been in the main that of building up churches, I know people are hungry to hear what God has to say, not what the preacher thinks, but what God has revealed of His mind and will through the person of Jesus Christ. People do not want sermonettes lasting ten minutes, although ten minutes from some preachers is ten minutes too long; nor do they necessarily want long discourses lasting for one hour. Some few outstanding men can do that, but very few. But a sermon that will last twenty-five to thirty minutes is usually within the capacity of the average preacher and the average congregation. This has been my pattern and practice. In the goodness of God I have seen churches grow under that kind of preaching, some from a handful of faithful folk to sizeable congregations. In Cockfosters we found it necessary to have two evening services every Sunday to hold those who came. For the last twelve years of my ministry, in a day when city churches were closing for lack of numbers, it was my privilege to preach to a well-filled church, both services being attended by hundreds including a high percentage of young people under thirty years of age.

I have letters from all over the world, almost every week, asking for help in the task of preaching. I make no claim to be a great preacher! Too many of the books on preaching are written by preachers of such outstanding ability that it is hopeless for the ordinary man to attempt to reach the heights to which these books call them. Maybe these messages of mine, which God has in His mercy been pleased to bless, which are the product of a ordinary preacher, will encourage other preachers, and at the same time speak to the hearts and needs of ordinary folk who crowded to hear the Master when He was on earth and who today will still crowd to hear what He has to say, and to see what He, in His risen power, can do, to meet and satisfy the human heart.

I owe a debt to so many whose books I have read and at whose feet I have sat, but above all to the hundreds and thousands in countries all over the world who have sat and listened to what I have felt God has had to say. Not least to the congregation of St. George's Tron in Glasgow where for twelve years the people came in their hundreds and were kind enough to indicate again and again that God's Word had spoken to their hearts. To those who have prayed for me I owe the greatest debt of all and to them I am sure in the end will go the credit for anything that may have been achieved through the preaching of the Word.

G. B. D.

To My Parents
from whose lips
I first heard of
CHRIST

Contents

I

What happened in Bethlehem?

'The Word became flesh . . .' (John 1. 14).

WE LIVE IN a time when the miracle of the Incarnation is not merely being questioned in some quarters but denied. This is of course no new thing, but this denial undermines one of the basic aspects of our Christian faith, namely, that Jesus Christ was God Incarnate, both truly God and truly man. I want therefore to share with you three statements that are worth keeping in mind when we consider what happened at Bethlehem.

THE POSSIBILITY OF THE INCARNATION MUST BE ADMITTED: and this, on two grounds. First, on the ground of *the bounds of man's knowledge.* Let us face the fact that man does not know everything; man neither knows everything about this world, nor everything about God. To say that the Incarnation was impossible is to assume that man does know everything about both man and God which, of course, is absurd. The farthest that scepticism can go is to say that the Incarnation is improbable, and we shall have more to say about that in a moment. The bounds or limits of man's knowledge demand, then, that the possibility of such an event happening must be admitted.

Secondly, the possibility of the Incarnation must be admitted not only on the grounds of the bounds of man's knowledge, but also on the grounds of *the basis of man's knowledge*. It is a simple truth that revelation lies at the foundation of all man's knowledge. My knowledge of the world in which I live comes initially to me through my senses, and my senses are all instruments of reception. In gaining my knowledge, I am a recipient. Through the senses of sight, sound, touch and taste, I receive impulses from without, and these my mind then interprets. So knowledge in the spiritual realm, the Christian faith asserts, falls into line with knowledge gained in the physical and material realm. Namely, knowledge of the spiritual world comes through revelation. Here, then, is our first statement. The possibility of the Incarnation must be admitted. Here is the second statement —

THE NECESSITY OF THE INCARNATION CAN BE ASSERTED. Let's take our argument a step further and speak not merely in terms of a possibility, but of a necessity. I find that, wherever there is a belief in God, one aspect of this belief is that 'God is love'. Love is the highest attribute in man. If it be found in the creature it must surely be found in the Creator. The trouble is that those who say they believe in God and that God is love, then make that belief a cushion upon which their thinking proceeds to go to sleep without going on to work out the implications of this.

I would support the contention that the necessity of the Incarnation can be asserted on these two grounds. First, that *human love demands the making of such a revelation*. For one of the supreme and universal characteristics of love is that it seeks to reveal itself. Whether it be the love of a child for a doll, of a man for a maid, of a mother for a child, love seeks in word, in look, in deed, to express and reveal itself.

This is exactly what Christ Himself said about His own love in John 14. 21, 'he that loveth me ... I will love him, and will manifest myself to him.' If this self-revealing quality is true of human love, surely we have a right to believe that it will equally be true of divine love. The love of God surely must *seek* to reveal itself to those it loves.

But if human love demands the making of such a revelation, we can add that *human life determines the manner of such a revelation*. Such a revelation must surely be made in such a way that the mind of man can fully apprehend it. But what level of life can man fully apprehend, save his own? And so we face the simple but rational and reasonable argument that if the love of God wanted to reveal itself to men, God must somehow do it as a man. This immediately takes us into what we call the realm of the miraculous, of the supernatural. But what may seem supernatural or miraculous to man is not necessarily supernatural or miraculous to God. God's love longed to reveal itself, and has done so at that level of life that man can most fully understand – namely his own. So Christ was able to say, 'He that hath seen me hath seen the Father.' Adequately, if not completely, God has revealed Himself, God's love has expressed itself, in human form in Christ. The possibility must be admitted: the necessity can be asserted: then finally –

THE AUTHORITY IN THE INCARNATION MUST BE ACCEPTED. If God has revealed Himself in Jesus Christ both in word and in deed, then the authority of Jesus Christ must be accepted. The Scriptures of the New Testament phrase this in three tremendous words in the opening verses of the letter to the Hebrews, 'God ... hath ... spoken.' One of the earliest memories I have of broadcasting recalls one of the earliest, if not the first, of the Christmas broadcasts made by the British sovereign. King George V had spoken to the nation, and then being a father he addressed some words to the children, and he introduced his words by saying, 'Children, the King is speaking to you.' When you and I listen to the words of Jesus Christ we can say quite simply, 'God is speaking.' In Jesus Christ we face an authority that is absolute because it is divine. If that be so, then two things must be considered. First, *the folly that rejects the words of Jesus Christ.* How often we meet well-meaning but misguided people whose attitude to spiritual truth is, 'Well, this is the way I look at it.' They seem never to have taken the trouble to find out what is the way that God looks at it, and that is much more important. They may be quite sincere, but sincerity is not truth. In Proverbs 16. 25 we are told, 'There is a way that seemeth right unto a man, but the end thereof are the ways of death.' To substitute what I think for what God has said is folly indeed.

And so we consider finally, *the faith that responds to the word of Christ.* Faith is essentially a response, a response to what I have come to know of the person through his words or through his deeds. As I come to know the person so I come to trust the person. Faith is, of course, more than mere belief, it is a responsive and submissive trust, a dependence on, an obedience to, One who having revealed Himself to us, we have come to know. Many years ago a Jewess in America who had considered many other beliefs came ultimately to accept the Christian faith, and she wrote, 'In Jesus we know all of God we shall ever know, and in Jesus we have all of God we can ever need.' And so the Scripture puts it down on record in these words, 'The Word was made flesh, and dwelt among us (and we beheld his glory, the glory as of the only begotten of the Father) full of grace and truth.'

That is what happened at Bethlehem!

2

A prayer that changed a life

'Behold the handmaid of the Lord; be it unto me according to thy word' (Luke 1. 38).

THIS PRAYER IS very short; and it was prayed by a woman. Possibly only a woman would have had the courage to pray it. The setting and the sequel to this prayer lie behind the words in the Creed which many of us have taken upon our lips Sunday after Sunday, '. . . Conceived of the Holy Ghost, born of the Virgin Mary . . .' But I want to think about it, not from the theological point of view, but rather from the practical point of view, because I feel that the whole experience of Mary is in some way a reflection of the experience that is the intention of God for every Christian. I want to begin by noting –

THE PURPOSE OF GOD REVEALED TO MARY. 'And the angel said unto her, Fear not, Mary; for thou hast found favour with God. Behold, thou shalt conceive in thy womb, and bring forth a Son, and shalt call his name Jesus.' Think for a moment *how intimately personal* was the relationship behind the purpose of God. Before that unique relationship that God planned for Mary we can only bow in wonder – wondering both at the mystery of it, and also at the dignity that it conferred on Mary, that she should become the mother of our Lord. But stop for a moment and ask yourself: Is this relationship any more intimately personal than the relationship that God still purposes for His own in Christ, that we should open our hearts and lives to receive the same Christ to be our indwelling Lord and Saviour? Mary's experience physically was to be one lasting for a few holy and wonderful months; but the spiritual experience of the Christian today of the indwelling of Christ, is to be an abiding experience. 'Christ liveth in me' is the theme truth of the New Testament.

See also *how immediately fearful* was Mary's response to the purpose of God. 'When she saw the angel, she was troubled at his saying . . .' It is a strange but common reaction to the intervention of God in human life, that men are afraid of God. I am not going to try to understand just what lay behind the troubled mind of Mary, but I think I know a little of what lies behind the troubled and fearful hearts of men today when they face the impact of God's truth and will.

Most of us are afraid of any personal dealings with God, for two reasons. The first lies in the fact of our own unworthiness: for although we may resent what the Bible says about 'all having sinned and come short of the glory of God', we know it to be true. The second, and main reason, is our unwillingness to accept the authority that we recognise is inherent in God's will. We would rather go our own way, plan our lives to suit ourselves; we would rather follow the crowd. And so when we meet God in a personal encounter of the soul we are compelled, at least for the moment, to recognise His authority, and we hate to be caught out in the life of disobedience in which we are indulging. Yet surely it is a simple fact that the only relationship to God which is a right relationship is one of obedience to His will.

Now think with me further of –

THE PROBLEM FOR GOD RAISED BY MARY. How understandable was *the objection raised:* 'How shall this be, seeing
I know not a man?' Mary was justified in raising this physical problem, in view of the utter impossibility of this experience of which the angel spoke ever being hers so long as she
thought in terms of that which was humanly possible. I suggest that we want to watch the terms of our thinking, lest we
set the same limitation. This is a danger from which some
men still suffer; that of limiting the possibility of what God
can do, to the confines of human knowledge and understanding.

But follow the story and see how, the objection having
been raised, the Scripture speaks of *the operation required*:
and God had already planned for that. Listen to these amazing words that fell upon Mary's ears long ago – 'And the
angel answered and said unto her, The Holy Ghost shall
come upon thee, and the power of the Highest shall overshadow thee; therefore also that holy thing which shall be
born of thee shall be called the Son of God.' Mary asked
what you and I ask, How shall this be? How can the very life
of Christ come to indwell my very body, my very personality? The answer is the same. 'The Holy Ghost shall
come upon thee.' Read the opening chapters of the Book of
the Acts, and you will see that this is so. The Church of the
New Testament was made up of those into whose hearts and
lives the Christ had come to dwell by the Holy Spirit. The
whole message of the New Testament is based upon the release of the person, the power, the ministry of the Holy
Spirit in the lives of those who have believed in Christ, that
Spirit through whom the very life of Jesus Christ is
mediated into our lives.

Finally think of –

THE PRAYER TO GOD RECORDED OF MARY. 'And Mary said,

Behold the handmaid of the Lord; be it unto me according to thy word.' There are just two simple thoughts with which I would close. First, note *the submission offered in* this prayer. It is a simple prayer, but it is one of utter abandonment to the purpose of God . . . 'Be it unto me according to Thy word.' She was saying, in effect, 'Here I am; do whatever you want with me.' What submission is here! Is this the kind of submission you and I are prepared to offer to God? His purpose for our lives is that they should be indwelt by the life of the Saviour. 'Behold, I stand at the door and knock,' says Christ; 'if any man hear my voice and open the door, I will come in.' 'Be it unto me according to thy word.' Have you ever prayed such a prayer?

Think yet again of *the salvation secured* through this prayer. It is a staggering thought that, humanly speaking, without Mary's submission there would have been no Bethlehem, no Calvary, no Easter, no Pentecost, no Church, no salvation. How much turned upon her obedience, she never knew. But how much may turn upon your obedience – the salvation of others in your family, in your church, in your circle of friends! 'Behold the handmaid of the Lord; be it unto me according to Thy word.' Would you pray that prayer, and see just how the answer will change your own life as it, too, gets caught up into the eternal and redeeming purpose of God for the world?

> O holy child of Bethlehem,
>   Descend to us, we pray;
> Cast our our sin and enter in:
>   Be born in us today.

So run the words of one of our hymns. 'Be it unto me according to Thy word.'

3

Afraid – of Christmas!

Fear not . . .' (Luke 1. 30; 2. 10;   Matthew 1. 20).

'WISHING YOU A very happy Christmas.' How familiar the greeting, and how simply and sincerely it sums up all that Christmas has so often held for so many of us. Amongst the many memories of childhood surely few can be happier ones than the memories of Christmas, memories of the excitement of buying the Christmas presents, of hiding them until the great day, and finally of opening them; memories of the hanging of Christmas stockings and the finding of them in the morning with their odd and angular shapes and exciting contents; memories of parties, of Christmas trees and of Christmas cards. Yes, they all made a 'very happy Christmas'. And if there should have been snow and frost during the Christmas holidays, sledging and skating out of doors, plus the sound of carol singers, all these and much more beside make the canvas of memory glow with colour, warmth and happiness.

I want, however, to ask you to pause with me and think a little more deeply into the real experience that lies beneath all this. Christmas is more than sentimentality, more than happy emotion. Indeed, it is strangely suggestive that to many of those involved in the events of the first Christmas

their first reaction was one of fear, and that three times over
within the context of the first Christmas-tide the message of
God to those caught up into the mystery and wonder of the
Bethlehem story was 'Fear not'. This was the word of God to
the shepherds (Luke 2. 10); to Mary the mother of our Lord
(Luke 1. 30); and finally to Joseph (Matt. 1. 20). I want to
ask you to think with me on this strange and almost alien
note – alien, that is, to everything that speaks of 'a merry
Christmas', but not alien to the deeper meaning that lies in
the cradle of Bethlehem. For just as we think of the coming
of Christ into the world of long ago, so the heart of the
Christian message speaks of a similar coming of Christ into
the hearts of men today. The 'Fear not' of long ago still
speaks to men's hearts today. Let us recall, then –

THE WATCHERS OF THE NIGHT. 'And there were in the same
country shepherds abiding in the field, keeping watch over
their flock by night. And, lo, the angel of the Lord came
upon them, and the glory of the Lord shone round about
them: and they were sore afraid. And the angel said unto
them, Fear not; for, behold, I bring you good tidings of
great joy, which shall be to all people. For unto you is born
this day in the city of David a Saviour, which is Christ the
Lord.'

How familiar the story is! But why were they afraid?
Surely the root of their fear lay in the fact that it was a
spiritual world upon which they had stumbled that night.
Here was an *atmosphere which was alien*, and strange to
their everyday, workaday world. They felt awkward and ill
at ease in it. It is the same today. Put the man who is hail-
fellow-well-met among other men, into a church, and he
would become ill at ease at once. But why? Surely for both
the shepherds and modern man there was a sensing of an
authority in that very atmosphere, an *authority which was
absolute*. Men know perfectly well that if there is a God,
then the most important thing in the world for any man to

do is to find out what that God wants him to do, and then to
go and do it. But few attempt to do this. Rather, they try to
escape any real contact with God, because the last thing they
want to do is to find out what God does want. They want to
get on with doing what they want. To find God breaking in
upon their lives is too much like being caught out in the very
act of wrong-doing. But for the shepherds and for us there
can come also *the assurance that was arresting*. 'Fear not . . .
good tidings of great joy.' Part of man's fear lies in this, that
the very last thing men conceive about the religion of Jesus
Christ is that it is a joyous thing. But this is what lies at its
very heart. 'I am come that they might have life, and that
they might have it more abundantly.' So spake the Christ.
And how men today need that same assurance! Men are
more frightened of God than they are prepared to admit.
They are afraid that God is going to take the fun and sparkle
out of life and make it a drab and dreary thing. The reverse
is the truth. 'Fear not.' The spiritual world upon which the
shepherds had stumbled that night and upon which men still
stumble as unexpectedly and as unmistakably is a world of
reality which plans for man's truest and deepest joy. How
eager was the shepherd's response. 'Let us now go and see . . .
and they came with haste, and found.'

Let us recall also –

THE WONDER OF THE MAID. For Mary too, espoused to
Joseph, the events of the first Christmastide brought a reaction of fear. Here are the words that record it: 'In the sixth
month the angel Gabriel was sent from God unto a city of
Galilee, named Nazareth, to a virgin espoused to a man
whose name was Joseph, of the house of David; and the
virgin's name was Mary. And the angel came in unto her,
and said, Hail, thou that art highly favoured, the Lord is
with thee: blessed art thou among women. And when she
saw him she was troubled . . . and the angel said unto her,
Fear not, Mary, for thou hast found favour with God, and,

behold thou shalt conceive in thy womb, and bring forth a son, and shalt call his name Jesus.'

Mary's moment of fear had come long before that of the shepherds, and for a different and more intimate reason. If the fear of the shepherds had its roots in the spiritual world upon which they had stumbled, Mary's fear had its roots in the personal experience upon which she must enter. Think for a moment of *the relationship that God asked*. It was the most wonderful relationship that God could ever have asked of any woman, that she should be the mother of His Son; that she should bear in her body the very life of the Saviour of the world. Is it any wonder that a fearful awe swept over the mind of the maiden espoused to Joseph? But it is a very similar experience to which God calls us today. The message of the Christian Gospel is not just the message of a Saviour who died upon the cross for the forgiveness of sins, but the message of a risen and living Christ who would enter the heart and life that is open to receive Him. It is this personal and intimate experience of Christ that is the intention of God for the individual still: 'that Christ may dwell in your hearts'.

Is it any wonder that *the reaction God found* was one of fear: 'She was troubled'? Men are still troubled when they face the personal nature of a vital Christian experience. If religion can be kept institutional and ecclesiastical, formal and social, then that is all right, but the moment you press it, as it must be pressed to something personal and vital, men begin to be afraid. Sometimes they take refuge, as Mary seems to have done for but a moment, in the apparent impossibility of the thing. 'How shall this be?' And the answer to Mary then, and to men now, is the same: 'The Holy Ghost shall come upon thee.' The Christian experience is more wonderful than that ever known by men when our Lord was upon earth. That experience of Christ was an obviously limited one, physically and geographically. It was for that reason that our Lord said, 'It is expedient for you that I go away, for if I go not away, the Comforter will not come.' The coming of the Holy Spirit was to make possible a new relationship with Christ that had no such physical and geographical limits as His disciples had experienced while upon earth. The Holy Spirit was to bring into the lives of men the very life of the Christ, assuring them not only of His presence, but also of His power to enable and to deliver. It is this note that is struck again and again in the New Testament: 'Your bodies . . . the temples of the Holy Ghost.'

The relationship God asked, the reaction God found, and very wonderfully, *the response God got*. The prayer of Mary in giving her submission to the will of God is possibly one of the loveliest of all prayers in the whole Bible, 'Behold the handmaid of the Lord; be it unto me according to thy word.' Would you dare to pray that prayer now as you face the implications of the will of God for you: 'Be it unto me according to thy word'? What a transformed life yours would become, even as Mary's was transformed from that very hour.

Finally, let us recall –

THE WORRY OF THE MAN. The third 'Fear not' of the first Christmas experience came to Joseph, the one to whom Mary was espoused. St. Matthew records this in these words: 'Now the birth of Jesus Christ was on this wise: when as his mother Mary was espoused to Joseph, before they came together she was found with child of the Holy Ghost. Then Joseph her husband, being a just man, and not willing to make her a public example, was minded to put her away privily. But while he thought on these things, behold, the angel of the Lord appeared unto him in a dream saying, Joseph, thou son of David, fear not to take unto thee Mary thy wife: for that which is conceived in her is of the Holy Ghost. And she shall bring forth a son, and thou shalt call his name Jesus: for he shall save his people from their sins . . .

Then Joseph did as the angel of the Lord had bidden him, and took unto him his wife.'

Where did the root of Joseph's fear lie? Surely here in the social complications to which he was exposed that night. Think, for a moment, of *the tongues that were unkind*. How they would smear the name of Mary and of Joseph. Has it ever occurred to you that our Lord entered the world under the shadow of shame? The stigma of a child conceived out of wedlock would rest upon Him and his mother. The tongues of men, or of women, have not changed, and how cruel and frightening they can be! God's ways with Mary and Joseph, and their relationship to the unborn Christ that God asked of them, demanded a courage that would dare to face and defy social opinion. It was so then, it is so still today. If there were the tongues that were unkind, there was also *the truth that was unknown*. Joseph and Mary could not have shared the mystery with others. They would not have been believed. They would not have been understood. Their words would have been rejected with scorn. And it is so still. The world cannot and does not understand the mystery of the Christian faith. It will still, in its ignorance, misjudge and scorn the words of the Christian as fumblingly and blunderingly he takes his stand with the ways and will of God. But with Joseph there was *a trust that was unafraid*, and quietly and simply we read, 'He did as the angel of the Lord had bidden him, and took unto him his wife.' 'He did as ... bidden.' What courage lay behind that simple act. It is possibly true to say that cowardice more than anything else today, keeps men back from obedience to that which God demands of them, an acceptance of the person of Christ into their very hearts and lives. To the coward in each of us God says anew, 'Fear not.'

A happy Christmas! Well, I wonder if it is really so for men today who pause to think of what it really means. The Saviour who came into the world in the miracle and mystery of that first Christmastide, who came to die for the for-

giveness of sins, and who rose again so that by the Holy
Spirit He might still come to the hearts of men, that Saviour
confronts men still with the challenge of His intention 'to
save his people from their sins', and to do so by entering the
lives of those He died to redeem. 'Behold, I stand at the door
and knock: if any man hear my voice, and open the door, I
will come in.' Does that intention worry you? Are you afraid
of what it will mean? Or is your response going to be like
that of the shepherds who came 'with haste', or like that of
Mary, 'be it unto me according to thy word', or like that of
Joseph who 'did as . . . bidden'? If you would make this response in the light of the threefold 'Fear not' of the first
Christmas story, then why not make this simple and lovely
prayer yours today?

> Oh blessed Jesu, Holy Child,
> Make Thee a bed soft, undefiled
> Within my heart, that it may be
> A quiet place, kept for Thee.

4

Relationship without fellowship

'His parents ... supposing him to have been in the company' (Luke 2. 44).

WHEN I CONSULTED my commentaries, I found that the passage Luke 2. 41–66, has been described in an extremely significant way. Professor William Barclay, with whose theology I differ from time to time, writes of it as 'one of the supremely important passages of the Gospel story'. If that is so, it surely demands our careful consideration. Another commentator describes it as a passage of 'quite extraordinary interest', and that again is a suggestive evaluation!

This kind of evaluation may be attributed to one or more aspects of its contents that are of special significance. For example, it is the only glimpse that we have into what are called 'the hidden years in the life of our Lord'. We're told a great deal about the circumstances surrounding his birth – details abound on that; and when we turn to these details, let us not be afraid of the element of miracle and of mystery that we find there. The story of the birth of our Lord is full of miracle, full of mystery, which takes us clean out of our depth; let's not be surprised that it should be so. To think that man with his finite mind can plumb all the depths of

the activities of the Creator God is arrogance indeed; and to
discard as untrue something we just cannot explain or
understand is not merely arrogance, it is blasphemy! The
birth of Jesus Christ was of course a unique event, and I'm
not surprised that there is miracle and mystery surrounding
it, when in the language of St. John 'the Word became flesh'.
But after so much detailed information has been given about
His birth, a veil of silence seems to descend upon all that
happened between then and the beginning of His ministry.
A veil of silence is drawn across His boyhood and His young
manhood, and that veil is lifted only here, when Jesus, we
are told, was twelve years old, and according to Jewish tradition was passing out of childhood into manhood.

This passage is significant, I believe, not only because it is
the only authentic glimpse we have into 'the hidden years' of
our Lord's life, but also because here we have the first recorded words spoken by Jesus Christ, when He said to Mary
His mother and Joseph, 'How is it that ye sought me? Wist
ye not that I must be about my Father's business?' or, 'in
my Father's house?' as the RSV translates it (v 49). These
first recorded words are significant because they reveal that
Jesus Christ was perfectly aware of the fact that there was
something distinctively unique about Himself. You remember how Mary said to Him, 'Thy father and I have sought
thee sorrowing' – 'thy father' referring to Joseph; and how
courteously and gently but quite firmly and unmistakably
Jesus Christ at twelve years of age chides her and corrects
her, saying, 'do you not know that I must be about my
Father's business? Do you not know that I must be in my
Father's house?' Mary called Joseph his father; Jesus speaks
of God as His Father! And so it would seem that not only are
these the first recorded words spoken by Jesus Christ, but
right away back when He was twelve years old, Jesus Christ
knew perfectly well who He was. We don't know how early
that awareness of who He was came to Him, but at least we
do know that at twelve He did know who He was.

Of lesser significance are two other facets of the incident.
One is that every indication here suggests that Mary herself
was the source of Luke's information about what happened,
and therefore we are quite justified in assuming that Mary
herself was the source of all the other earlier information
that Luke has about the birth of Jesus Christ. If this information came from the lips of Mary the mother of our Lord,
I don't think she's likely to have made a mistake; mothers
have an incredibly accurate memory about details like this!
And the other less important aspect of this incident is that
here we have the last recorded reference to Joseph, sup-
porting the tradition that he died before our Lord's ministry
began. These are possibly some of the reasons why this passage is described as one of the supremely important passages
of the Gospel story, and a passage of quite extraordinary
interest.

But I want to view the incident recorded here in another
light, from another angle: to see here in the experience of
Mary – an experience of deep distress and anguish – a
reflection of the kind of experience that we too may well
know something about. If I were to take a text out of this
incident, I think I would pick the words in v. 44, 'Mary,
supposing Him to have been in the company', and if we were
to take a title to cover the thoughts that I want us to share
together, it would express the possibility of there being in
our lives, as there was in Mary's, 'relationship without fellowship'. Let us get a hold of that title, because this I believe
is the thrust of what you and I can learn from this incident –
the possibility of there being a relationship with Christ without fellowship. For at least three days Mary and Jesus lost
completely all contact with each other – something that, I
venture to suggest, had never happened in this way before.
Mary was still His mother; Jesus was still, according to the
flesh, her son; the relationship was there, but not the fellowship. In this story only three days were involved, although
they must have seemed like an eternity to Mary. In your

experience and mine three days could be three years, thirty years in which we have had a relationship with Jesus Christ, but no fellowship with Him. The thrust of what we're going to examine is that it is possible to be a Christian and yet at the same time to be right out of touch with the Lord – right out of touch. Relationship, yes; that hasn't changed, but fellowship exists no more.

I want to look at Mary's experience and see here the kind of experience that can be ours. First of all I want to notice what I've called –

A LIFE THAT HAD BEEN FOUND – a life of fellowship with Jesus Christ. For twelve wonderful years, first in Nazareth when the Annunciation came, then in Bethlehem when Christ was born, then back in Nazareth for almost the entire period of those twelve years Mary's life had been so closely intertwined with His life; every day and all day He had been there. She had been with Him and He had been with her. A life that had been found.

Think of *the wonder of the companion she would find in Him*. Mary knew perfectly well who He was, as far as it was possible for her finite mind to grasp divine truth. The words of the angel Gabriel were fixed on the walls of her memory and they shone there as if they had been written in gold; she would never forget what he had said. Do you remember the words, 'The angel came in unto her and said, Hail, thou that art highly favoured, the Lord is with thee: blessed art thou among women ... Fear not, Mary, for thou hast found favour with God. Behold, thou shalt conceive in thy womb, and bring forth a son, and shalt call his name Jesus. He shall be great, and shall be called the Son of the Highest: and the Lord God shall give unto him the throne of His father David; and He shall reign over the house of David for ever, and of His kingdom there shall be no end'? Mary never forgot her trembling response, 'How shall this be, seeing I know not a man?', nor the answer that came to her, 'The

Holy Ghost shall come upon thee, and the power of the Highest shall overshadow thee: therefore also the holy thing which shall be born of thee shall be called the Son of God.'

Yes, Mary knew who He was, and so do you; so do I. She would never forget that moment when she came to see her cousin Elizabeth; you remember that when Elizabeth heard the salutation of Mary, her babe leapt in her womb and Elizabeth was 'filled with the Holy Ghost; and she spake out with a loud voice and said, Blessed art thou among women, and blessed is the fruit of thy womb. And whence is this to me, that the mother of my Lord should come to me?' Nor would Mary ever forget how, when Jesus was just six weeks old, she had taken Him up to the temple, and what had happened when Simeon took Him in his arms; nor would she forget what had happened when Anna the prophetess had taken Him into her arms. Yes, Mary knew who He was. Whether as a babe in her womb, as a babe at her breast and in her arms, as a child in her home, she knew that Jesus was the Son of God. What a companion she would find Him to be! But what Mary had in her home, Christians have in their hearts in an even closer relationship. She knew who He was – the Son of God. Oh, the wonder of the companion Mary had known Him to be!

Then think of the wonder of *the communion that Mary would have with Him.* Not only would He be there, but how much they would do together; how often they would talk together! How much there would be kept locked away in Mary's heart! We're told again and again that she did this; she locked things away in her heart and then she pondered over them constantly. With such a son and such a mother the fellowship must have been wonderfully deep, a growing and deepening experience as He grew, as we are told in 2. 40, 'The child grew, and waxed strong in spirit, filled with wisdom: and the grace of God was upon Him.' Tell me, has this not been the very heart of what it has meant in your life and mine to be a Christian? It means not only that we have a

Saviour, but we have a companion; and when we think of the companion that He is, when we think of the communion that we know, it has not simply been a matter of having Him there, it has been a matter of sharing so much, sharing everything indeed with Him. The things that have been done together, the thoughts that have been shared together: Mary knew all that for twelve years! How long have we known it? How many years have passed since Christ was born in our hearts by the Spirit? In our early Christian experience, fellowship with Jesus Christ, the companionship of Jesus Christ, the friendship of Jesus Christ, has been our unbelievable privilege and delight – it has meant everything to us to have our life shared with Him and His life shared with us.

A life that has been found: we can see it here. Mary had found it, she had known it for twelve unforgettable, wonderful years – the Son of God in her home. Perhaps there is somebody reading these words who is not a Christian. You need to know that that is what being a Christian is all about; it means literally having the Son of God by the Spirit of God not in your home, but in your heart: a new life, a new presence, a life that can be found. Have we all found it? Or are we still messing around with the scaffolding inside which the true church grows? Are we still taken up with ordinances, with attendance at services with creeds and even conduct, and have nothing to do with Jesus Christ? A life that can be found. It can be found now if we have not found it before.

Then secondly, I see as I get beyond the twelve years –

A LOSS THAT SHOULD BE FEARED. Something happened! In all probability it was the first time that Jesus had been back to Jerusalem since He had been a little baby of six weeks. He was now twelve years old, when according to Jewish custom and tradition He had attained manhood and therefore had to meet the obligations of the law in His own person, one of those obligations being attendance at the Passover. So now He's back in Jerusalem, Joseph and Mary having taken Him there. I can't help wondering what thoughts filled His mind during those days. We don't know how long they stayed; it was required that they should stay for at least two days during the period of the main sacrifices, though the Passover feast lasted seven days. The suggestion has been made that, like some who lived at a great distance from Jerusalem, Mary and Joseph left after the two or three days; this is suggested by the fact that the doctors of the law were still in the temple for spiritual counsel and instruction, which they gave right throughout the Passover. So it is possible that the caravan set out for Nazareth half-way through the seven days of the Passover because they had further to go. Apparently the custom was that the women would set off first, followed later by the men who might travel faster; both parties would then meet at night, and camp for the first night's stop. It was then that Mary and Joseph discovered that Jesus wasn't there. A loss that should be feared. The relationship remains; but now fellowship just doesn't exist!

I wonder whether this message is for somebody about whom there is no question at all as to whether or not you are a Christian. You can tell me the very day when you became one, and you can tell me some of the things that happened in the early days of your Christian experience. But if you were honest, you would have to tell me one other thing, and that is that you have absolutely no fellowship with Jesus Christ now – none at all! The relationship is still there; of course you're a Christian; but fellowship doesn't exist. And so we read that they had journeyed 'supposing him to have been in the company'. But when they sought him among their kinsfolk and acquaintances and they did not find Him, they 'turned back again to Jerusalem, seeking him'. I wonder if you would have to be just as thorough and absolute in your statement that if you were to go round your life right now, you wouldn't be able to find any real evidence of the reality of the presence of Jesus Christ in your heart by His Spirit. You never hear His voice; you never feel His touch on your

life; you never see His face. Relationship – yes; fellowship –
no!

A loss that can be feared. And we see here first of all what
I've called *the carelessness through which she had lost Him.*
Perfectly understandable it may well have been; Mary assumed possibly that Jesus was with Joseph, Joseph assumed
possibly that He was with Mary, but neither of them *made
sure* that He was there. No check was made, no enquiry;
they just supposed Him to have been in the company; they
took it for granted that whatever they did or didn't do Jesus
would still be with them, and He wasn't!

Some of us who call ourselves Christians think we can do
what we like and it won't have any effect on the fact that
Jesus Christ is with us. Well, it won't alter the fact that He's
there, but it may have the most profound repercussions upon
our fellowship with Him. What a foolish assumption to
make! Fancy Mary making this kind of assumption! Fancy
Joseph making this kind of assumption! I wonder why it was:
was it the sheer 'busyness' of the day? Was it because there
were so many people to talk to, so many people to meet?
Was Mary busy talking over the experiences of the Passover
feast? So taken up with her experiences, and talking to
people about them, that she forgot her son? All I do know is
that it is possible for us to become engrossed in our experiences, and even in the services of the Church, to become so
obsessed talking to people and thinking that *that* constitutes
fellowship with Him, that we lose sight altogether of the
person of Jesus Christ. We've got plenty of time for the
Church, we are never absent on a Sunday; but when were
you last alone with your Bible? When were you last alone
with your Lord? When did you last listen to *Him*? Plenty of
time for the Church, but no time for the Christ. And suddenly we waken up and discover that we can't see His face,
we no longer hear His voice, no more do we feel His hand in
our lives. The constancy of His presence nothing can
change; the consciousness of His presence anything can

change! They lost Him ... not through anything terrible; they hadn't done anything terribly wicked; but just, I think, through sheer busyness and carelessness they lost touch with Him.

The carelessness with which she had lost Him; the *ceaselessness with which she now looked for Him.* Three days, we're told, she searched ... three days of agony, of tramping the dusty roads, with a terrible fear gripping her heart that she might never see Him again. Some of us have been to Jerusalem, and have been in great crowds there. The city would be thonged with tens of thousands of people; and with a boy of twelve lost in that, Mary's heart would be wrung. First of all she went among her kinsfolk and acquaintances. I wonder what she said to them. Of course she told them that she was looking for Jesus, but I wonder if she attempted to excuse herself; I wonder if she was looking for sympathy; I wonder if she wanted them to tell her that it wasn't really her fault at all. But she didn't find Him there.

Sometimes when you and I are out of touch with Jesus Christ, that's precisely what we do. We go and talk to our kinsfolk and acquaintances; we go and talk to our friends; and although we may admit things are not right or as they should be, all the time as we talk to them we're trying to make out that it is not really our fault, it is somebody else's. We are looking for sympathy, for understanding. I want to say to you that Mary and Joseph did not find Him among their kinsfolk and their acquaintances and neither will you. You can talk to your friends until Doomsday, and you will never, *never* find Him! No, not there!

Then they did what they should have done before; they went back to Jerusalem. One of the most difficult things in the world sometimes is to *retrace our steps*: but they went back! I would say to you that there comes a time in the life of every one of us when, if we are going to find Jesus Christ, we have to retrace our steps and admit that we have gone the wrong way and *in* the wrong way. They went back to the

place where they had last seen Him, where they had lost
Him. No, not right away; they didn't go first to the temple,
and that was foolish. It did not take them three days to get
back there. No: they searched the streets, they searched the
houses, they searched the markets. How slow we are to come
to the place where we lost Him; how slow we are to come to
the point. Then finally they went to the temple where they
had last seen Him, and there they found Him – found Him
exactly where they had left Him.

That is where you will find Him too – where you lost Him,
where you left Him. When things began to go wrong with
your spiritual life of communion with God and fellowship
with Jesus Christ, when the peace went, the sense of His
presence went, His voice went silent, His book went dumb,
and everything in you of the Spirit just seemed to die out, do
you remember when your trouble actually started? Well, get
back there; you will find Him. However long it may take us,
we have got to go back to where we went wrong. Do you
remember the words to the Church at Ephesus in Revelation
2. 5, 'Remember therefore from whence thou art fallen, and
repent and do the first things'? In other words, get back, get
back to where you were? Get back! Retrace your steps.
Admit you have gone the wrong way. Admit you have blundered. Get back ... to where you lost Him. The loss that
should be feared. I cannot imagine anything more terrible in
the Christian life than to know what it is to have had fellowship with Jesus Christ for twelve years (less or more it
doesn't matter) and then through some carelessness, some
stupidity, suddenly to find that He is not there! He is there
of course factually, but not consciously. Do you remember
how God said long, long ago concerning His people, 'Eph-
raim is joined to idols, let him alone.' In other words, God is
saying concerning His people, 'They know perfectly well
that that is forbidden, but if they are determined to go that
road, I'll let them go, and let them find out the consequences
of departing from my will.'

A life that can be found; a loss that should be feared; and
finally –

THE LORD THAT MUST BE FACED. They found Him – yes,
they did. 'It came to pass, that after three days they found
him in the temple, sitting in the midst of the doctors, both
hearing them and asking them questions. All that heard him
were astonished at his understanding and answers. And
when *they* saw him, they were amazed: and his mother said
unto him, Son, why hast thou thus dealt with us? Behold, thy
father and I have sought thee sorrowing. He said unto them,
How is it that ye sought me? Wist ye not that I must be
about my Father's business?' – or, 'that I must be in my
Father's house?' The Lord that must be faced.

I suggested, by way of introduction, that in these first
words spoke by Jesus Christ, He makes known to Mary,
absolutely unmistakably, but very gently and chidingly, very
carefully and courteously, exactly who He is. 'Son, why hast
thou thus dealt with us ... behold, thy father and I have
sought thee sorrowing.' Jesus replied, 'Do you not know that
I must be about *my* Father's business?' 'Do you know who
you're talking to? You're talking to the Son of God. That is
who I am.'

The Lord who must be faced. Two final considerations are
here. First, *the thoughts revealed in what she said*. When
Mary speaks, is there not a hint of rebuke, based upon a way
of thinking about the relationship between her and Jesus
Christ, that failed altogether to take into account the nature
of the Person to whom she was speaking. 'Why hast thou
thus dealt with us? Behold, thy father and I have sought
thee sorrowing.' Had Mary forgotten who He was? Had
familiarity bred, if not contempt, certainly forgetfulness?
The thoughts revealed in what she said.

The truth recalled in what He said. What Jesus Christ
said recalled her to something she already knew, and that
was simply that she was speaking to the Son of God, and it

was with the Son of God she had to deal. 'You really did not need to search for me,' He said. 'Where else would you expect to find me but in my Father's house, occupied in the concerns of my Father? You speak to me as if I were but Joseph's son; you know that I'm not; you know who I am; you know who *my* Father is. I am the Son of God, and therefore above all question, above all rebuke, above all fault-finding. Please be to me and with me what you have so consistently been for so long. Don't take up this attitude towards me, and all will be well.' The Lord that must be faced.

I wonder whether God has caused some of us to consider this because the one thing that we need above everything else, if fellowship with Jesus Christ is going to come back into our lives, is to come face to face with Jesus Christ Himself and thrash things out with Him; not with your friends, but with your Redeemer and your Lord. How do you think the things you have said to excuse yourself would sound in His ears? Have they any weight there? Or would Jesus Christ have to say to you what He said to Mary, 'What on earth are you doing, talking like that? Have you forgotten who I am? Have you?' Then having drawn back the curtain to give her just a glimpse of His true nature, He drew it back again, and we are told that He went down with them to Nazareth, and was subject to them. I like to think that the experience of the first twelve years was renewed, that Mary never forgot again who He was. He was the Son of God, that boy who helped about the house as He grew into young manhood, and, if it is true that Joseph died, that son of hers who took the burdens off her back and kept the family, the Son of God and Lord of Glory!

I wonder if you have forgotten who Jesus Christ is. He was born in your heart and life by the Holy Spirit, I don't know how many years ago, and for so many years you had wonderful fellowship with Him, and then something went wrong. You have not been able to find Him, no, you have not, not for years. He's brought you to this moment because He wants to recall to you something you have forgotten: that Jesus Christ really is the Son of God, and the One before whom you and I must bow the knee. It does not matter what anyone else says or thinks, or what we say to anyone else; it is what happens between Him and you and Him and me that counts. I don't think Mary ever forgot again! I wonder whether you will. Let us remember, then, the possibility of having relationship without fellowship, of living a life that is out of touch with your Lord. In one of S. D. Gordon's books I came across a poem that has stuck in my mind, and I quote it as I close.

Only a smile, yes, only a smile
That a woman o'er burdened with grief
Expected from you, 'twould have given relief,
For her heart ached sore the while;
But weary and cheerless she went away
Because, as it happened, that very day
You were *out of touch* with your Lord!

Only a word, yes, only a word
That the Spirit's small voice whispered 'speak';
But the worker passed onward, unblessed and weak,
Whom you were meant to have stirred
To courage, devotion and love anew,
Because when the message came to you
You were *out of touch* with your Lord!

Only a note, yes, only a note
To a friend in a distant land;
The Spirit said, 'Write', but then you had planned
Some different work, and you thought
It mattered little. You did not know
'Twould have saved a soul from pain and woe:
You were *out of touch* with your Lord!

Only a day, yes, only a day,
But oh! Can you guess, my friend,
Where the influence reaches and where it will end
Of the hours you have frittered away!
The Master's command is 'Abide in me';
And fruitless and vain will you be,
If *out of touch* with your Lord!

5

The temptation of Christ

'Then was Jesus led up of the Spirit into the wilderness to be tempted of the devil' (Matthew 4. 1).

ALL THREE GOSPELS, Matthew, Mark and Luke, record the temptation of Jesus Christ, and I like to believe that His temptations were real. Later on in the Epistles we are to be told that 'He was tempted in all points like as we are, yet without sin' (Heb. 4. 15). But when we consider the temptations of Jesus we face a dilemma, for if He was truly God, as we believe He was, then He could not sin; but if He could not sin, then He was not truly man, as we also believe He certainly was! I like to think that the temptations of our Lord were real, and that when He was meeting temptation He faced it as man, holding if you like His deity in reserve, putting it to one side and not drawing upon His divine resources to cope with His temptations. A similar situation might arise if the son of the owner of a great factory entered the factory in order to gain experience of it, beginning at the bottom, and although he was the son and indeed the heir who one day would own the factory, yet had chosen to work his way through just as any other workman. So I like to think that when our Lord faced His temptations, whether here or in Gethsemane or the final temptation on the cross to come down from it, the temptations were real, and He met them and conquered them as one who though God was truly and wholly man.

I believe there is a great deal that we can learn from the temptations of Christ, and especially the temptation mentioned in Matt. 4. I want to consider what we can learn from His experience so that we may know what we may expect in our own life of obedience to the will of God. Of course, in some ways His experience was unique, but there are, I believe, some basic principles and similarities between His temptation and ours. Let us begin by noticing what I have called –

THE SIGNIFICANCE OF THE MOMENT. What a wonderful moment had just passed in the life of our Lord: the moment of His baptism, when in the previous chapter we read that the Spirit had descended upon Him in the form of a dove, and how the voice of the Father had been heard saying, 'This is my beloved Son, in whom I am well pleased.' It had, of course, been a moment when publicly and deliberately He had identified Himself both with the need of man in his sinfulness and the will of God in its redemptive purpose. It had been then for Him what we might call *a moment of resolve*. In v. 13 of the previous chapter we are told that He came specifically 'to be baptised of John' in Jordan. We have the recorded protest of John in v. 14, that 'John forbad him, saying, I have need to be baptised of thee, and comest thou to me?' These words would indicate that in John's eyes this was no usual baptism; it was not like any of the other countless baptisms that John had performed: and yet our Lord insisted that He Himself, who we know to have been without sin, should be baptised of John in what was called a baptism of repentance, even though He had no sins to repent of. Whatever else His baptism meant, surely it meant His formal declaration of His acceptance of the destiny that was His in the redemptive will of God for Him and through Him for the world, and that He was identifying Himself with the sinfulness from which mankind needed to be cleansed, and of which mankind needed to repent. It was, if you like, an act of dedication, of consecration, of high resolve, in which He set Himself apart for the destiny which was His. He was committed now to do the work He had come to do. It was, if you like, a crisis of commitment, a moment of resolve.

For each of us, too, there can come such a moment when we have come to a clearer realisation than ever before of what the purpose and the will of God might be for us, and we in a similar identification of ourselves with God's redemptive purpose in the world have responded with a similar resolve to say 'yes' without reserve to all that the will of God may hold for us. We are familiar, as believers, with the need of decision on the part of unbelievers – that initial decision to turn from self-reliance to faith in a crucified and yet risen and living Lord. But the Christian is not finished with the need for making decisions after that first and initial one. Constantly we, too, face similar moments in which a clearer understanding of the implications of our obedience to the will of God challenge us to a new, a fuller and deeper commitment.

Sometimes these decisions may be made in some great convention such as that held at Keswick in the Lake District each July, where some seven or eight thousand Christians from all over the world gather for a week in which to study the Word of God and to bring their lives into a closer alignment to the will of God found there. Indeed, one of the great teachers at the Keswick Convention in its earlier years used to say that while a conference was a place for discussion, a convention was a place for decision. And how many decisions by Christians have been made at conventions like Keswick or Filey which have led to a total involvement in the will of God. Indeed, it would be true to say that the time spent in such conventions would have been wasted had there been no such decisions. The decisions might have been made in the area of repentance, something that obedience to the will of God meant putting out of our lives or maybe something to be brought into our lives. The decisions may have been in the area of obedience and of a surrender of ourselves totally to Him, a willingness to recognise God's right to control every part of our lives, a willingness to accept that will whatever its demands might prove to be. Or it could have been a decision in the area of faith or of trust in the light of all that God has promised and provided for us in the person of His gracious Spirit. We were brought to the point of being willing to believe in God's faithfulness as well as His fullness, and so to place ourselves without reserve in His hands and allow the Holy Spirit to work out His own ways in our lives, to make ourselves utterly available to God for whatever His purpose and will might ask.

But it was also *a moment of response*. We read immediately that 'when he was baptised ... the heavens were opened unto him, and he saw the Spirit of God descending like a dove, and lighting upon him: and lo a voice from heaven, saying, This is my beloved Son, in whom I am well pleased.' The response was a divine response in which there was both a vision and a voice. Many years ago, before I ever had the privilege and responsibility of preaching from the Keswick Convention platform, as a young Christian I heard the late Bishop Taylor Smith pray at the opening meeting of the convention, that we at Keswick might be prepared for a vision and a voice. In the case of our Lord, the Spirit of God appeared in the form of a dove. A dove is the symbol of peace; and what is peace? Someone has said that peace is the possession of adequate resources. Is it not wonderful when God in His mercy reveals to us that in our union with our risen and living Lord by the Spirit, we too have adequate resources; a sufficiency of grace to meet our every need, and that has brought us in a very real way an assurance and a

peace to our hearts. We realise that in a deeper measure we
are accepted by our Lord. Fellowship and communion with
Him become more meaningful. Our spiritual sight somehow
or other seems to be clarified, and our spiritual sensitivity in
hearing God's voice becomes more real, as we too have experienced our moment of response. And so we notice the
significance of the moment.

But no sooner has the moment passed than we have the
words, 'Then . . . the devil'; and so the second thing which
has something to say to us concerns what I have called –

THE IMPORTANCE OF THE MAN. 'Then was Jesus . . . tempted
of the devil.' I want us to consider *the choosing of the target*.
The choice of the target was the one Man through whose
obedience to the will of God salvation would be made available to the whole world. Jesus Christ had indicated by His
baptism His acceptance of His destiny, and in doing so had
at that same time thrown down the gauntlet at the feet of
the devil himself. I trust and hope that we believe in the
existence of a devil! There are some people who do not believe in a real devil, although not so many in these days in
which there is so much dabbling in the occult. The number
of those who disbelieve must be small indeed! What a strategic place Jesus held in the redemptive purposes of God, and
surely it was because of this that the devil tempted Him. If
he could defeat Jesus, then the whole place of salvation
would be in ruins.

Of course, Jesus Christ was uniquely strategic: the salvation of the whole world depended on His obedience; but
to a much lesser degree, yet in a very similar way, you and I
are strategic! Every one of us is different, and in that sense
every one of us is unique. We are different in the per-
sonalities we have which God wants to use. We are different,
too, in the circles of lives that we touch and that God wants
to reach through us. Someone has said that 'every Christian
lives at the centre of expanding circles of contact' and God's

way is to reach men through men, and God made your personality one that would touch lives that could not be
touched through any other personality. God wants to reach
certain lives through your life, and others through mine. He
could never reach these lives without us; He needs us, and so
do the people He wants to reach through us. It is just because we are different that we are strategic, and it is because
we are strategic that we are tempted! In war the attacks that
are launched against the enemy are at the strategic areas;
the factories, the bridges, the railway lines, the air bases.

But we do well to note not only the choosing of the target,
but *the channels of the temptation*, and we note how varied
these can be. At first the devil appealed and tempted our
Lord through His natural and physical appetites, in suggesting the making of stones into bread. This is one of the ways
in which he still continually tempts Christian people,
through our physical appetites, through our physical in-
stincts; and the more powerful the instinct the more likely
he is to appeal to it: He will do anything to divert us from
the will of God! Someone indeed has said that if the devil
can't keep us from being converted, he does his best to see
that we are diverted!

Another channel was used when he tempted our Lord
along the line of social acclaim and popularity, when He was
taken to the pinnacle of the temple to do the popular thing,
the spectacular thing. Surely again this is one of the channels
that the tempter uses constantly to get us to conform to the
pattern and the standards of an ungodly world. How he
longs to get in to compromise our lives for the sake of being
popular with men! In the book of Proverbs we read that 'the
fear of man bringeth a snare', and how many Christians
have forfeited the pleasure of God for the sake of pleasing
society.

The third channel that the tempter used was related to
material advancement, when the devil promised to give to
Christ all the kingdoms of the world if only He would fall

down and worship him. How many Christians have fallen
when tempted along this line, for the sake of material gain.
They have compromised their obedience to God like Demas,
a companion and fellow labourer of St. Paul, who forsook
Paul, 'having loved this present world'. How many Christians for the sake of financial gain have deliberately dis-
obeyed the will of God!

So the devil will probe the whole area of man's life to try
to find a point of weakness that will lead to a yielding to
temptation. In the case of Jonah the temptation came along
the line of his patriotism; in the case of David the temptation came along the lines of his sexual desire; in the case of
Paul the area of danger was his tired-out and exhausted
body – so he cried out, 'I keep under my body lest I should
be disqualified.' So we note the importance of the man as
well as the significance of the moment.

There is one more thought: which I have called –

THE RELEVANCE OF THE MESSAGE. I believe that there are
two final lessons we can learn as we witness the temptation of
our Lord. The first is that there is *no need to despair*. Most
of us find temptation depressing beyond all words; we feel
that we must be very wicked indeed to be tempted, very
sinful! It seems as if the devil never leaves us alone, will
never give us a moment's respite. But all the time the real
reason that we are tempted is not at all because we are very
wicked. Christ was not wicked, He was without sin! The real
reason that we are tempted is therefore because we are very
important; and why are we important – because we are so
strategic! I wonder if this is why we are told in James 1. 2,
'Count it all joy when ye fall into divers temptations.' The
only Christians who should be depressed are those that are
never tempted, those Christians for whom life goes along
smoothly and without incident! It surely means that if they
are not tempted then they are not important, they are not
worth bothering about; they count so little for God and

therefore matter so little to the devil, that he leaves them alone!

So the first lesson is that there is no need to despair; in fact, the harder the battle the more we should rejoice – and that is surely what James says further on in the chapter, where we read, 'blessed is the man that endureth temptation', and you know that the word 'blessed' is simply 'happy'. Happy is the man that endures temptation; and if we are to endure it, then we must of course encounter it. So I would suggest that we can rejoice in a very real way when temptation beats in upon us; it means that just as the devil will not leave us alone neither will our God! So there is no need for despair; temptation is not sin, indeed it is the evidence that Satan wants to make us sin, which is a very different thing.

That leads me on to the second tremendously encouraging thought that we can take to ourselves from this aspect of the temptation of Christ. If there is no need to despair, there is also *no room for defeat*, for here we see demonstrated the victory of the Lord whose life we share. 'He was tempted in all points like as we are, yet without sin.' You know the story of the Negro who was asked if now that he was a Christian he had the victory over the devil. 'No,' he said, 'I haven't got the victory, but I have the Victor,' and this is the note that runs right through the New Testament. Do you remember how Paul writing to the Romans says, 'Now in all these things we are more than conquerors through Him that loved us' – 'in all these things': there is no area where we need suffer defeat, because there is no area where our Lord suffered defeat. Again, Paul writes to the Philippians, 'I can do all things through Him that keeps on pouring His power into me' – so runs one translation. Here in His own temptation we see just a glimpse of the victor at war, we see Him triumphing over the enemy and doing so wonderfully and convincingly, and that victor is our Saviour and our life. Many years ago when I was a young Christian I came across a booklet entitled *The Life that Wins*. The impression made upon me by the opening sentences in that booklet has lingered in my mind ever since. Built upon the words of St. Paul in Phil. 1. 21, 'To me to live is Christ,' the writer said that there is only one victorious life and every Christian has that life, and that life is Christ's life being lived out in us by His Spirit. When I went to the Keswick Convention as a young Christian the young people's meetings were under the leadership of the late Mr. A. Lindsay Glegg. One of the choruses that we sang was titled 'On the Victory Side', and the words went like this:

> On the victory side,
> On the victory side,
> No foe can daunt me,
> No fear can haunt me,
> On the victory side . . .
> With Christ within
> The fight we'll win,
> On the victory side.

'The fight we'll win' – Christ and I! Having Christ we have all we need to defeat the enemy, and so there is no room for defeat and no need for despair!

6

The life transformed by Him

'She said, If I may touch but his clothes, I shall be whole' (Mark 5. 28).

EVERY MIRACLE IS surely but a parable in action, and here we have a miracle which sets out a truth that I believe to be important: that the purpose of God for each of us in Christ is not only that we should have spiritual life, but that we should have spiritual health. This woman was alive, but not well. Jesus said, 'I am come that they might have life, and have it more abundantly.' But today we see all around us a Church that is spiritually sick, and Christians that are very far from living lives that are spiritually what God meant them to be.

How often when friends meet the usual question is asked, 'How are you?' To which the usual untrue reply is made, 'Very well, thank you.' I wonder, if we should meet the Lord and should hear Him saying to us, 'How are you?' What would our reply be? In the early days of the Revival in Ruanda in Africa a frequent greeting from one Christian to another was, 'How is your heart in the Lord today?' There is an old-fashioned hymn that is sometimes sung with great fervour, but I sometimes shrink from singing it, where in the chorus it is affirmed, 'It is well with my soul.' But is it really well with our souls? Let us face the fact that it is possible to have spiritual life without having spiritual health; but surely health is God's purpose, and should always be our purpose too. The prophet Isaiah brought this very same charge against the people of God in his day. He said, 'The whole head is sick, and the whole heart faint. From the sole of the foot even unto the head there is no soundness.'

Let us look, then, at the incident when health came to one who was sick. There are three points I would like to make, and I trust that these may clarify the direction of our thinking together. First of all we see here –

A LIFE FROM WHICH HEALTH HAD GONE. 'A certain woman, which had an issue of blood twelve years, and had suffered many things of many physicians and had spent all that she had and was nothing bettered, but rather grew worse ...' Note *the presence of a crippling disease*. Twelve years she had been sick, and that is a longish time; but I wonder how long some of us have been living in spiritual ill-health. What about our spiritual appetite? Is our appetite for the Word of God healthy? Those of us who have small children will know that a loss of appetite is an indication of ill-health. When our children turn away from the plate of food in front of them we say, 'Hello, what's the matter with you?' So, what is our spiritual appetite like? And what about our hearts? Our love for the Lord? Our love for the house of God? Our love for the world that God loves? How much caring is there in our lives; and with the caring, giving too? And what about our breathing? Sometimes we may find ourselves sitting next to someone whose breathing is not quite right, and we know immediately that there is something wrong with them. What about our praying? Our spiritual breathing? Is that all right? And what about our tongues, our testimony?

One of the first things a doctor says when we are not well

and have gone to see him is, 'Can I have a look at your tongue?' What about our tongues? Is there a good testimony there as to what Christ has meant to us? I am not asking, 'Do we know the Gospel?' Of course we know the Gospel; but if we were present in a testimony meeting, have we an up-to-date living testimony on our tongues? Or is our tongue more often filled with frivolous, unkind or unworthy words? What about our temperature, is that normal? Or is our temperature a bit high? Are we inclined to lose our temper? Or maybe it is a bit below normal; do folk find us unfriendly and cold? What about our skin, our appearance? Sometimes we can tell by the very look of a person, by the condition of their skin, that they are not well. Are we so obviously spiritually well that we don't really need to tell anyone we are Christians: they can tell it and see it? Here is a woman who has been sick for twelve years with a crippling disease. How long some Christian lives are tragically below the standard set out in God's Word!

I note also *the pressure of a crushing despair*. At least this woman wanted to do something about it! She was ready to go anywhere, to listen to any voice, to pay any price to anybody if only she could find health. All we are told is that she had suffered many things from many physicians, and had spent all that she had and was nothing better – although Dr. Luke omits, 'But rather grew worse'! If ever a life was utterly bankrupt and crushed into despair, this woman's life was like that.

I wonder if some of us are just in that state. We are just where this woman was. We are not only spiritually sick and living below the level of God's intention and provision, but we are absolutely at the end of our resources. We have tried everything, read every book we can; we have listened to preachers, gone to church, gone to great conventions. Well, a great Christian like Paul knew what it meant to be brought to the end of his tether, so we are in good company. Do you remember how he wrote in 2 Cor. 1. 8, 'At that time we were completely overwhelmed, the burden was more than we could bear, in fact we told ourselves that this was the end' (J. B. Phillips). I wonder if you have ever found yourself to be just like that – at the last gasp. We really seem to have reached the very bottom. Every possible remedy has been tried, and it has failed. Every bit of effort has been fruitless! This woman was bankrupt. Paul was like that, but he added, 'We believe that we had this experience of coming to the end of our tether that we might learn to trust in God.' I had a book sent to me the other day and the very title was suggestive: it was called *Crowded to Christ.* For if this was a life from which health had gone it was also –

A LIFE IN WHICH HOPE WAS BORN. We read in Mark 5. 27, 'She heard of Jesus.' She came in the crowd, in the press, and touched His garment, for she said, 'If I may touch but his clothes, I shall be whole.' And so here was a life in which hope was born, and I pray that this day will be a day in which hope is kindled in your heart and mine, for don't we need hope today?

What did all this mean? First, it meant there had to be *a learning of Christ.* Reports reached her of Jesus, of what He said, of what He did, of what He asked, and what He could do, and what she heard of Him brought a ray of hope into a dark sky. I believe that at the root of many of our problems today in the Church at large there lies a basic ignorance about Jesus Christ. God's charge in the days of the prophet Hosea was, 'My people are destroyed for lack of knowledge,' and the Church today desperately needs to learn what Christ has to say, what He claims to be able to do, what He wants us to do, and how He wants us to live. We are told in Rom. 9, 'Faith cometh by hearing, and hearing by the Word of God.' God has no time for ignorance. Faith is not a feeling, it is a response to truth heard; and faith and hope will begin to kindle in our hearts as they kindled in the heart of this woman when we hear as she heard of Jesus! That means for you getting down to your Bible, in your home, and for me getting down to my Bible in mine. It means being in our place in church twice on Sunday, not once in the morning and then in the evening lounging in front of our television set watching a play. It means getting to a Bible study, if there is one; and if there isn't one it might mean starting a Bible study group in our own home. We simply have to learn about Christ; there is simply no substitute for this kind of basic knowledge of him.

How tragic it is that there is so much ignorance – and as a minister I have to be fair here, for ministers and the clergy have to accept their share of responsibility for this too. On holiday recently I went to a service on a Sunday morning, and I went with a hungry heart. But when it came to the time when the Word of God was to be preached, the minister lounged back on one elbow in the pulpit, chatted away for five minutes, and then finished, and we were sent away, empty and hungry. There are of course some rather pathetic people who say that a sermon must not be longer than ten minutes. Poor creatures! They send their little five-year-olds to school, and the lessons that these little five-year-olds have to go through are longer than ten minutes, and they have more than one lesson a week. A Roman Catholic leader in Holland said, 'Things will begin to happen when we begin to take Jesus Christ seriously', and that means we have got to start learning about Him.

Have you not been frightened sometimes, when you have seen on your television screen a documentary from China, and watched tens of thousands of Chinese young people, holding in their hands the book that they knew off by heart? A book that does not bear comparison in its worth with the book that you and I have. But we neither have our book in our hands nor in our handbags, nor in our pockets, nor in our minds. Most of us know almost nothing about it. 'When we begin to take Jesus Christ seriously.' This means learning.

What this woman heard of Him was not much, but it was

a starting point, and it was enough to create something else, for here there was not only a learning of Christ but also *a longing for Christ*. 'If I may touch but His clothes,' she said, 'I shall be whole.' What she had learned, she had believed; and what she had believed she then wanted to see happen in her own life. With a passion and purpose she was determined to reach Him and touch Him, and while the multitudes were thronging Christ, she was touching Him. Many years ago, in Portstewart, in Northern Ireland, at a great convention held in that lovely part of the world, I heard a great preacher speaking on this incident, and one little phrase that he said has stuck in my mind. He said, 'The flesh throngs, but faith touches.' There are so many people who throng around Jesus Christ; you will find them in every church every Sunday, but out of the many who throng there are few who touch Him. I wonder how many hands of faith are reached out with intention and purpose to touch Him, every Sunday, every day. Hearts that are longing to tap the resources that are in Him, and to relate those resources to their needs. So many people today are interested in Jesus Christ. They are curious about Him. Indeed, maybe they enjoy the services they go to, but there is no real desire, no intention, no resolve, no determination to relate what He is and what they are and what they need. Not so with this woman. A learning of Christ was followed by a longing for Him. She said, 'If only I could get within range of Him, and reach out and touch His clothes I know I shall be whole.' I trust that we are learning enough about Christ to make us long for Him. Here we have, then, a life from which health had gone, and the life in which hope was born. But finally we can see here –

A LIFE FOR WHICH HELP WAS FOUND. We read, 'Straightaway the fountain of her blood was dried up, and she felt in her body that she was healed of that plague. And Jesus immediately knowing that virtue had gone out of him, turned

him about in the press and said, Who touched my clothes?
And his disciples said unto him, Thou seest the multitude
thronging thee, and sayest thou, Who touched me? And he
looked round about to see her that had done this thing. But
the woman fearing and trembling, knowing what was done
in her, came and fell down before him and told him all the
truth. And he said unto her, Daughter, thy faith hath made
thee whole; go in peace, and be whole of thy plague.' So
here we have a life for which help was found. We can learn
from these final touches in this miracle two further important truths. The first is that *what Christ gives must be received personally*. So we see Christ isolating this woman who
has the touch of faith, from the thronging crowd; and we
need to remember that what Christ can do, what Christ will
do, He will do personally and individually. In the psalms
there is a wise piece of counsel which stresses the need for
individual and personal faith. The psalmist says, 'My soul,
wait thou only on God,' and if we are to meet with Christ in
a meaningful way it must be a personal and individual encounter. One of the great American preachers once said that
a sermon to be a true sermon must be an event. It is something that is not just heard, but something in which there is a
happening. And what is that happening? Surely it is a personal encounter and an involvement between an individual
and the Master.

'Somebody hath touched me.' That is what Jesus said in
Luke's account. Here is a personal confrontation with
Christ. Those who criticise the Billy Graham type of crusade or who criticise other great gatherings of Christians
overlook one tremendous spiritual fact, which is that the
Holy Spirit can isolate an individual in a crowd, just as Jesus
did with this woman. And if I know anything about great
gatherings from the experience of something like forty years
in the ministry, this is exactly what can happen and what
does happen! People will find themselves somehow or other
in a situation where as far as they are concerned they feel as

if there is nobody else there in the crowd but themselves and their Lord. What Jesus gives, then, must be received personally.

And what Jesus does must be revealed publicly. In other words, what Christ does in us and for us is not something that we are to keep to ourselves, it is something that others are bound to know about and indeed to see. And in that knowing and in that seeing all the glory will be given to Him. St. Luke's account reads that, 'She declared unto him before all the people for what cause she had touched him, and how she was healed immediately.' The people then went away not thinking what a wonderful experience this woman had had, but what a wonderful person Jesus Christ was.

So here we can see the story of a life from which health had gone, a life in which hope was born, and a life for which help was found. And if for some of us there is to come a new experience of Jesus Christ which will transform us by His grace, we shall have to be honest, we shall have to bear our witness to the Christ who has met our need, and let others know that it is Christ who has done it. We are living in a world which is absolutely filled with clamouring voices. It seems as if the only voices that are not heard are the voices of those who have experienced Christ's saving grace. We never bother to write to the BBC or ITV to tell them we don't want their kind of muck and filth shoved into our homes under the guise of art. We don't write to the papers, we don't lift up our voices in the office. Everybody seems to be doing the talking except believing Christians. We stay dumb and silent. But Jesus said to this woman, 'What has happened to you is something which you must let others know about, because otherwise you will get the glory, and the glory is mine.' I wonder how many times the angels surrounding the throne and close to the presence of the risen, ascended and enthroned Lord hear Him whisper to Himself, 'Somebody hath touched me.' And as the hand of faith goes out to Him, and as you and I lay hold of Him in all His fullness, we can then go on to live for Him in a new and fuller way, and bring glory and praise and honour to His name.

It is possible to have spiritual life: have you got that? Have you been born again? But have you got spiritual health too? Many years ago at a convention in Leicester I remember hearing the late Rev. W. H. Aldis saying that he had just received a telegram from a gathering of Christians in China. This was in the days when China was free. And in this telegram they said they were praying for the Church – not that they should be better Christians, but that they should be 'well' Christians! There is all the difference in the world between better and being 'well'. Are you a 'well' Christian? Have you got the spiritual life and the spiritual health that Jesus Christ can give?

7

The lives He didn't use and the life He did

'Wilt thou not revive us again, that thy people may rejoice in thee' (Psalm 85. 6).
'Oh that thou wouldest rend the heavens, that thou wouldest come down, that the mountains might flow down at thy presence' (Isaiah 64. 1).

DURING MY WORLD travel and ministry in many lands, the conviction and conclusion to which I am driven is a simple one, namely this: that the supreme need of the Christian Church today is for revival, for a movement in power of the Spirit of God that will both cleanse and energise the Church of Christ everywhere. I want therefore to study with you what a former Keswick speaker, Dr. S. D. Gordon, once called 'The Sychar Revival' as recorded in John 4. I believe that there are lessons here to which the Church would do well to pay heed. First of all I find –

A WARNING HERE THAT IS ALARMING, and the warning centres around the simple fact that the disciples of the Master seem to have had little to do with what happened in Sychar that eventful day. In v. 8 we read of their arrival in the city, but as far as one can judge their arrival caused not a ripple of interest in the city. Consider then, *the tragedy they must represent* – the tragedy of being by-passed by the Spirit of God, of being left out of this great experience. After all, they were the disciples of the Master; they had both a position and a prominence that would have led people to believe that they would be in the very centre of anything their Lord was planning to do: but they weren't, they were left on one side, while the stream of blessing flowed by on another course.

What a warning we find here for those of us who profess and call ourselves Christians; what a challenge lies here for those of us who hold office in the Church, who hold positions, it may be of greater or less prominence, for those who are ministers or bishops, elders or deacons. Are we likely to be in such a movement of the Spirit of God, or are we going to be left on one side? The verdict of history, as well as the record of the Scriptures, warns us again and again that when revival touches the Church, the movement seems to leave on one side the very people we would have expected to be in the heart of it.

But consider also *the opportunity they never sensed*. We might well ask why? Why was it that the disciples were so by-passed when such a work was to be done? Does the Scripture here give us any answer? There are two verses that hint at possible reasons: in v. 8 we read, 'they were gone into the city to buy meat' – a very necessary and legitimate concern, but was it possible that bread for themselves occupied their minds to the exclusion of blessing for others? Were they too preoccupied in these legitimate and necessary but material things even to sense the need all around them? I wonder if that was it, *preoccupation*? All I know is that today it is tragically true that too many Christians are so preoccupied with material and social matters that they have no time to sense, let alone minister to, the spiritual needs around. No time for the prayer meeting at the church, no time to give to the winning of others to the Master. Is pre-occupation the cause?

Or was it something else then – is it something else now? In v. 9 we read, 'the Jews have no dealings with the Sam-aritans' – preoccupation; or was it *prejudice*? Had the dis-ciples washed their hands of the people that God had planned to bless? Prejudice – is that still a characteristic of the Church? What about the attitude of many Christians to the unconverted folk around, the neighbour next door, the people they work with, that girl in the office – have we already made up our minds that God has no intention of doing anything there: they are too hard, they are not in-terested, they are so worldly; and so, like the disciples, we pass by the opportunity that God has planned to grasp and use.

Whatever the reason, then in history, or now, the warning that strikes a note of alarm in my mind is that it is possible, only too possible, to find that the disciples are left out. Should revival touch the Church of Christ where you are, would you be in it; would you welcome it, or would the Spirit of God pass you by on the other side? Yes, there is a warning here that is alarming – but there is more: there is –

A WONDER HERE THAT IS ARRESTING, and the wonder lies in the instrument God used. If the arrival in the city of the disciples caused not a ripple of interest, the arrival of the prostitute woman threw the whole population into a ferment of excitement, and in minutes the whole city was streaming out to meet with Christ. The wonder of this revival, like any other in history, was first of all, *a wonder of grace*: compare the disciples, after all, with the prostitute! No one would have had any doubt as to which instrument God would use – the disciples, obviously: but no, they would have been wrong; it was the woman that God used that day. A wonder of grace; not only a woman, but such a woman – a prosti-tute!

Has it not always been so? Has revival not always had as its instruments the unlikely, the unworthy? Read for yourselves not only the Sciptures but the history of the Church, and see how again and again the principle is found exemplified that 'God hath chosen the foolish things of the world to confound the wise; and God hath chosen the weak things of the world to confound the mighty; and base things of the world, and things which are despised hath God chosen, yea, and the things which are not, to bring to nought things which are.' How absolutely true, and how absolutely thrilling – for this brings hope to all of us who feel our unworthiness, who know ourselves to be such ordinary people: if God could use such a woman as that then, could He not use such a Christian as myself now? A wonder of grace.

But it was more than that: it was – *a wonder of power.* The instrument used that day was no doubt unexpected, but it was not unprepared: the woman was not just a prostitute but – can we doubt it? – a prostitute who had found a place for repentance. The woman who startled a city, who set the people marching out to meet with Christ, she was a changed woman. The power of Christ had changed her; but in that very transformation two things had found a place in her experience. The first was *penitence.* 'Go, call thy husband' – she had been faced with her sin. There is still an ethical pre-requisite for revival. Who was it that said that the vessels God uses need not be of gold or silver, but they must be clean?

Is it true today that the only thing that holds up revival is the unrepented sin of the Church? Was it Finney who said that 'revival consists in a new obedience'? Let us recognise that Christ did not come to destroy the law, but to fulfil it. Thank God, grace has replaced the law as far as our standing before God is concerned: we are not justified by the works of the law; but nor are we absolved from its demands in Christian living. Possibly one of the greatest needs within the Christian Church today is such a facing up to the ethical

pre-requisites for revival as will bring us to the place of repentance.

Yes, penitence found its place in the preparation of the
instrument — and *prayer*. 'Give me' — and what an
intensity of desire must have gone into that prayer. 'If thou
hadst known thou wouldst have asked . . .' said the Master,
and then unfolded such a picture of what He Himself could
be that her heart cried out for it. If lack of penitence be part
at least of that which hinders revival, is lack of prayer the
other part? Is this the other great failure of the Christian
today? It was this penitent and prayerful heart that was so
transformed so that a whole community was startled and
arrested, and compelled to ask, as others were to ask later,
'What meaneth this?'

A warning here that is alarming; a wonder here that is
arresting; and finally —

A WORK HERE THAT WAS ABIDING. The last arrival in the city
was the arrival of the Master Himself. Consider *the preacher
they heard*. 'We have heard him ourselves,' they said to the
woman. Is there anything more desperately needed today in
the life of the Church, and of the Christian, than a listening
to the word of the Master? How desperately those who seek
to lead the Church need to recognise that they themselves
must acknowledge the One who is the Head of the Church.
The charges that the Master brought against the religious
people of His own day are charges that He could still bring
against the Christians of today. Do you remember His
words, 'Ye have made the Word of God of none effect by
your tradition,' and again, 'Ye have taken away the key of
knowledge; ye entered not in yourselves, and them that were
entering in ye hindered.' 'It is written, my Father's house
shall be called the house of prayer, but ye have made it . . .'
What? A new listening to the voice of the Master is surely
what we need. We need to meet with God; to expose our
lives to the searchlight of God's truth. They were able to say,

'We have heard Him ourselves.' Can you say that? Can our ministers and leaders say that; can the members of our churches say that – 'We have heard Him'?

'Yes, that was the preacher they heard; and that was *the presence they knew*. We read, 'He abode there.' Revival surely is not more and not less than the presence of Jesus Christ in the soul. It is the practical implication of this fact that we need so desperately to work out. The cry of the Old Testament prophet was that 'the mountains might flow down *at thy presence*'. Nothing less than this will do; and this by itself will be enough.

'Wilt thou not revive us again, that thy people may rejoice in Thee.' May the story of the Sychar Revival yesterday become your story and mine today!

8

The woman who knew His forgiveness

'Neither do I condemn thee: go and sin no more!' (John 8. 11).

'THE FRIEND OF sinners' was a taunt hurled at Christ with the contempt of His foes: now it is a title treasured by the millions who own Him as their Lord. Christ's right to that title is unforgettably set forth in John 8. 1–11, telling how He was confronted with the woman taken in adultery. I have been trying to get in my own heart a clear vision of the Christ who met the woman that day, and who is always ready to meet with us. There are four thoughts which I want to share with you now. Notice in this incident, first of all –

THE FAIRNESS OF JESUS. We are all familiar with the fact of the silence of Christ when the woman was brought into His presence. We know too, that there has been a lot of speculation as to why, after the charge was made, Christ wrote in the ground and as to what He wrote. I am not going to enter into speculation, but I want you to notice that the fairness of Jesus *did not permit him to deny the charge.* He was fair to the men who brought the woman; He was fair to the woman they had brought; and He was fair to Himself. He did not deny the charge. Note that. Let us not try to deny such charges as circumstances may bring against us. Christ does not.

But the second thing I notice in the fairness of Jesus Christ was that He *refused to limit the charge*. The accusers of the woman wanted it limited to one woman and to one sin, and Jesus would not have it that way. He looked at the men and said, 'He that is without sin among you, let him first cast a stone.' They wanted to limit the charge to one sin and one person; but Christ was absolutely fair, and He wanted each person present to know the fact of his own sin and his own kind of sin. It may be that as some of us listen to sermons about sin, we may say to ourselves, 'That does not touch me.' But will you remember that Christ does not limit the charge. We may have been saying to ourselves, 'I am not that kind of person.' Listen: 'He that is without sin among you, let him first cast a stone.' I wonder what would happen in our churches if this incident of long ago could be re-enacted again; I wonder, how many of us would be left in the building. The fairness of Jesus! Thank God, He is absolutely fair! But notice also –

THE TENDERNESS OF JESUS. Something had to happen; there were *the people that had to leave*. Some had to go from the scene before Christ would or could go any further, and these were the men who had brought the woman in. You see, she had been in very close touch with them; she had got their angle on the situation, and she knew exactly what they thought. Christ wanted to get them out of the way. When you and I are conscious of sin, I would suggest to you that there are times when we are far too conscious of what men say about us, of what men think about us, of how others evaluate us. Before Christ can get anywhere with us, He has almost always got to get people out of the way. In the matter of our sins there is nothing the Church needs so much as for you and for me to get man's evaluation of sin out of our minds. Jesus could not and would not deal with her before the men. They had to be out of her sight and out of her thoughts.

But while the Scripture states the fact that certain people had to leave the scene, the record also speaks of *the people that then were left*. I do not know if any of the folk standing around were looking now. I should be very surprised if any of them were, for I read this, that 'Jesus was left alone with the woman.' Some, I think, had turned to look in other directions; others were just looking at the ground, while others had no doubt left the scene. For all practical purposes Jesus and that woman were left alone – just the two of them, the sinner and the Friend of sinners. If I am going to have my sin dealt with, I want it dealt with there.

'Jesus saw none but the woman.' He saw the woman! I am sure that it was on the ground of what He saw that the story unfolds so wonderfully, and goes on to record –

THE FORGIVENESS OF JESUS. I wonder *what did He see*? I wonder what Christ sees in you and me in relation to our sins? Does He see in us what He saw in the woman that day? I wonder if He saw tears on that woman's cheeks? Did He hear her muffled sobs as she lay there, crushed and crumpled in the dust? I wonder if He saw right into her heart, and found there a desperate hurt and pain and grief? What did He see; and *what did He say*? Note, will you, the way He spoke to her: 'Woman' – it was a term of affection, a word of complete courtesy. We do not know what His tone was, but I rather think it would have been a tone of infinite kindness – 'Woman, where are those thine accusers? hath no man condemned thee?' And the woman accepts His emphasis on the standard which His words suggest, and answers, 'No man, Lord.' The fairness of Jesus is matched by the tenderness of Jesus; but both lead to the forgiveness of Jesus. She knew that no man could condemn her after what Christ had said; they had all gone; no man could condemn her, but

God could, Christ could. How unexpected was the word that she next heard, 'Neither do I condemn thee' – not now. I might have condemned you when you were first brought to me, when the charge was made; but now that we have got rid of the men, and now that I have seen you, and now that I know your heart, 'neither do I condemn thee'.

How unexpected! How unlimited! God's forgiveness is so different from man's. We forgive people and then we do not want to have anything more to do with them. If God forgave sin like that, He would not have anything more to do with anybody! But God's forgiveness is unlimited. How often we take the 'all' of the Word of God and say 'all but', and there is an 'all' concerning the forgiveness of sin – 'If we confess our sins, he is faithful and just to forgive us our sins, and to cleanse us from all unrighteousness' – not 'all but', but 'all'. The fairness of Jesus, remember that; the tenderness of Jesus, remember that; the forgiveness of Jesus, remember that.

And last of all, I see here –

THE HOLINESS OF JESUS. 'Go, and sin *no more*.' Remember that! Christ made it quite clear that *her sinning had to stop*! Christ was not excusing her sin or condoning it; but with equal certainty He had no intention, now that she was down, of keeping her down, of trying to make her sin something that would be a hindrance to her all her life. At the same time, He wanted to make quite certain that what happened that day was real and sincere and final.

The time may come in our lives when we are convicted about some sin about which Christ has spoken to us – remember, He did not limit the charge to one kind of sin – and now He wants to say to us concerning that sin, 'Go, and sin no more.' But surely He meant also that *her living could now start*; for Christ was not suggesting that she was going to an impoverished life, a difficult life, to one that was ruined for ever. I cannot understand the attitude of mind of some Christians who have a message of forgiveness for the unconverted sinner, but no message of forgiveness for the converted sinner; and, alas, that attitude is far from uncommon today! It may be that you have no experience of forgiveness to offer to a Christian who sins, whereas for the unconverted person who has gone very far into sin you have a message of forgiveness, and indeed his experience becomes a kind of showpiece of what God's grace can do! Why do you not offer the same measure of forgiveness for that same sin in a Christian?

We forget sometimes that there is a war on, and that when there is a war on we expect people to be wounded. But surely when they are wounded we give them every care and the very best attention that we can. And when men are killed in battle and go down into the mud and blood, we honour them for the devotion that took them there. Don't let us forget that there is a war on for the Christian, and there will be wounds and blood; there will be tears; there may even be death. Yet, thank God, moving through the battlefield is the Saviour Himself, and He brings to us the healing that we need, the forgiveness that we need, the grace and the mercy that we need; all that we need. I wonder if His word to you or me today is, 'Go, and sin no more'?

Shall we take the pen from the hand of Christ and write across the record of whatever sin there may be in our lives, just two words – 'no more'? It will mean that finally and for ever we are finished with it. We have played with it long enough; but, recognising the holiness of the Jesus whose forgiveness we so desperately need, we are going to write across the record, hitherto unfinished, of that sin in our lives – 'no more'. I love the words of that hymn –

> O hope of every contrite heart,
> O joy of all the meek,

To those who fall, how kind Thou art!
How good to those who seek!

Listen with me as Christ speaks to us now, 'Neither do I condemn thee' – not now; oh, yes, once I did, but not now. 'Go and sin no more.'

9

Some who did not want Him

'Then the whole multitude ... besought Him to depart from them: for they were taken with great fear' (Luke 8. 37).

IN THE TEACHING of God's Word we come always to face up to the sovereignty and lordship of Jesus Christ, and the obedience motivated by love which is the only right relationship to Him. Yet I think it is at this very point that many of us begin to become afraid. A well-known American preacher has written that 'people want to be saved, but not from their sins. They want to be saved, but not at too great a cost. They want to be saved, but in their own way.' This incident from the New Testament brings home to us that there can come a point when Jesus Christ becomes unwelcome – 'Then the whole multitude ... besought Him to depart from them; for they were taken with great fear.' And there can come a point in our own experience when Jesus Christ is not welcome, in the total of what His person means and involves. It is the possibility of our rejection of Christ in a certain aspect in our lives, that I want us to face. Because it is possible that in some of our hearts and lives there is building up a sense of resistance to the authority and claim of Jesus Christ as Lord of our life. So I want to look at this incident; and I find here three things which I think are relevant to our present age and our own lives. First I find –

DISORDER IN THIS COMMUNITY TO WHICH CHRIST CAME. Things were not right. It was a community that was uneasy, and more so than might appear on the surface. But first let us look at the obvious factor in the situation, which would seem to have been the immediate concern of Christ. He was concerned with *the helplessness of man* – this devil-possessed man, and of the community in which he lived. We read in v. 27 that 'there met him outside the city a certain man that had devils long time, and wore no clothes, neither abode in any house, but in the tombs'. Mark's account adds, 'Neither could any man tame him, but always night and day he was in the mountains and in the tombs, crying and cutting himself with stones.' And Matthew's account adds, 'No man might pass by that way.' Here was a man whose life was enslaved to evil; and that enslavement and helplessness constituted a threat to the community. He was not only constantly hurting and damaging himself, but he was liable to hurt others: a life dominated by forces that men seemed powerless to curb. 'No man could bind him, no not with chains.' And it would seem as if our Lord's first concern was with the helplessness of this man; threatening the community, hurting himself, and liable to hurt others.

This is surely one of the very patterns in our modern scene, that make life for many people uneasy. We live in an age of wonder – there is no question about that: wonder at the scientific achievements of men today, this amazing space age, this atomic age. But is this not equally true, that if this is an age of wonder is it not also an age of worry? The obvious question that is continually thrusting up its head is, What is the good of man conquering space, if he cannot conquer self and sin? And was there ever a time when evil was so blatant or so beastly, as evil as it is today?

Some little time ago this aspect of our modern age was focused sharply for me when I was asked to address a meeting of undergraduates in Trinity College, Dublin, and they gave me the subject, 'Has Man a Future?' As I faced the challenge of this subject and the question it raised, I suddenly realised that today whenever I face a group of young people, I face a generation that has no guarantee whatsoever that it will be allowed to grow up. The so-called advance of man's scientific knowledge has created for the first time a situation where man's mere survival on the earth is now a debatable and dubious question, and that the total annihilation of human society and civilisation as we know it is a menacing and murderous possibility.

But for most of us the sense of hopelessness, the sense of worry and anxiety, the threat that overshadows life, is of a more intimate character. We wonder what will happen to our children growing up in this age. What will happen to home life as we knew it. What will happen to the Church of God, to the whole Christian pattern and standard of living. This threat of untameable and uncontrollable evil is a desperately urgent and ever-present one: 'no man could tame him.' Christ was concerned; and concerned with this element of disorder in the life of the community to which He had come – the sheer helplessness of this man's enslavement, the hurt he was to himself, and the threat he was to the community.

This was the obvious aspect of Christ's concern; but then there emerges another area of Christ's concern. We find coming into the area of the concern of Christ, *the wilfulness of man*. For although this region of Decapolis was one of mixed race and religion, the historian Josephus tells us that those involved in this incident with the herd of swine were Jews, and that being so they were deliberately disobeying the law of their God. For reasons which maybe we do not understand, the pig to the Jew was an unclean beast, and no Jew was allowed to have anything to do with pigs. Yet here were

Jews openly and deliberately disobeying their God; not only doing it, but making money out of it. Was it their distance from Jerusalem that made them feel they could get away with it? Or was it possibly that the pagan environment around them made them feel it would be all right? Others did it, why should not they? But I wonder if there was an undercurrent of uneasiness, a sense of guilt that was carefully concealed but lay closer to the surface than possibly others realised. There was a spiritual and moral disorder running right through the lives of many in this community. I wonder if I'm right in suggesting that today we are living in an age when the distinctions between the Christians and the pagans are becoming increasingly blurred, that basically there is a principle of disobedience to the Lord and of conformity to the world that is having some strange results.

Christ today, as then, is concerned not simply with our helplessness, but with our wilfulness. I wonder if this is because of the distance between us and Jerusalem? Is the Christian Church failing to live as close to God as once it did? Is there disorder in our lives today – the disorder through man's helplessness which is obvious, the disorder though man's wilfulness which is less clearly discerned? I often recall that lovely hymn of Bishop Handley Moule which begins with the words, 'Come in, O come . . .' the second verse runs –

Alas, ill-ordered shows the dreary room;
The household stuff lies heaped amidst the gloom,
The table empty stands, the couch undressed;
Ah, what a welcome for the Eternal Guest!

Yet welcome, and tonight; this doleful scene
Is e'en itself my cause to hail Thee in;
This dark confusion e'en at once demands
Thine own bright Presence, Lord, and ordering hands.

The disorder of life: the ordering hands of Christ. I wonder whether we are ready; I wonder whether we really want His ordering hands?

The second word I want to share with you is –

DISTURBANCE FOR THE COMMUNITY TO WHICH CHRIST CAME. For into this scene of disorder and confusion came the Master; and whenever and wherever He comes, the whole scene changes. Christ introduces a new element into any situation. He came and changed the whole picture, because of the dual capacity in which He was presented.

First *His adequacy is seen.* The enslavement of this man to evil was broken; and nothing is surer than this, that the power of Christ is adequate to cope with all the forces of evil in the human heart. We believe, surely, that 'if any man be in Christ Jesus he is a new creation'. We believe that when Paul said, 'I can do all things through Christ who strengtheneth me', he was stating the truth. We believe it to be true that 'in all things we are more than conquerors through Him that loved us'. And when the Gadarene folk came out to Jesus, we read, they saw him that was possessed with the devil 'sitting clothed, and in his right mind'. The adequacy of Jesus Christ to deal with our helplessness is indisputable. 'He is able to save to the uttermost all who come to God by Him.' This was the purpose of His coming: 'Thou shalt call His name Jesus, for He shall save His people from their sins.' The adequacy of Christ to deal with our helplessnessness is surely something that is basically true. If He cannot save us from our temper, what kind of a Saviour have we to offer to the world? If He cannot save us from thoughtlessness or selfishness, from unreliability, from jealousy and envy, what kind of a Saviour is He? He is no Saviour at all. The whole testimony, the whole message of the New Testament Gospel, is that 'He is able to save.' And His adequacy to deal with man's helplessness is seen here. I hope it is seen in your life and mine. And so it was that the people of Gadara found themselves confronting a power that was greater than any human power: and nothing is more needed today than this kind of testimony to the power of Christ. Yet we read that when they saw the man sitting, clothed and in his right mind, they were disturbed.

But that wasn't all: if Jesus Christ was only One who was able to deal with man's helplessness, then He would be most welcome. If it was simply that I could demonstrate His adequacy, that would be wonderful. But not only is Christ's adequacy seen, but *Christ's authority is sensed*. These men who heard the story of the deliverance of the maniac and the disappearance of the herd of swine instinctively linked the deliverance of the maniac with the loss of their living. If it had been just a matter of Christ removing the threat to their safety by healing the maniac, that would have been all right; He would have been welcome. But when Christ started interfering with their way of life and their means of livelihood, that would never do! When Christ started challenging them on the question of their total obedience to their Lord God, they didn't want that, and panic seized them.

You see, sin can be uncomfortable; and when I'm made uncomfortable by my sin, it is nice to be relieved of discomfort! But sin isn't just something that is uncomfortable: sin can be sociable; sin can be profitable; and when I find that Jesus Christ is not only concerned with delivering me from the power of sin – certain sins in my life that are distasteful, or even dishonouring to Him – when I find that His authority is linked with His adequacy, and He seeks to take over the control of the whole realm of my life, I begin to kick at this.

Let us face it, there are certain areas in our life that we don't want Christ to interfere with. The Lordship of Christ, the authority of Christ is everywhere apparent in the Bible. I wonder whether, if you and I were to bring our lives in their wholeness into the presence of Jesus Christ, we would find to our amazement that Christ's purpose would not simply mean dealing with those things concerning which we are helpless, but would mean dealing with certain other areas of our lives concerning which we would not wish Him to have anything to do. It could be in the realm of our business. Someone said that sin pays as well as pleases, and it's true. Sometimes you and I want God to deal with the sins that are inconvenient to us, the sins that make us uncomfortable, the sins that make us ashamed; but if Jesus Christ is going to so permeate our lives and so exercise his adequacy and authority that He is going to make us different from other people, that really is taking things too far.

I wonder whether there is any real difference between you and your colleagues at the office in the way you talk, the interests you have, the ambitions you share, the language you use, your pursuits, hobbies and recreation. If I were to come and work in that office, would I be able to pick you out as a Christian right away? In that hospital, in that staff room, in that university commonroom, in that hostel, at that wedding reception? Would you stand out as a Christian? Immediately? Or are you prepared just to experience the saving power of Jesus Christ and His adequacy in those areas of life that are disturbing and distressing to you?

I believe that this is the crux of the problem today: we all want to be saved from certain sins, but we don't want Jesus Christ to be Lord of our lives, Lord of our money, Lord of our time, Lord of our relationships. There are so many of us like that would-be disciple who said, 'Lord, I will follow Thee, but . . .' I remember Dr. Graham Scroggie telling of an incident in Charlotte Chapel many years ago. After a service there was somebody in grave distress, whom he sought to counsel. He sat alongside this lady, and found she was fighting this very question of the Lordship of Christ over the whole of life, and there was one area that she was not prepared to yield. Dr. Scroggie turned over the pages of his Bible, and asked her to do the same; they came to the place where, in Acts 10, we read of the vision that Peter had, of a great sheet let down from heaven, and in it all kinds of beasts. And a voice said, 'Rise, and eat,' and Peter said, 'Not so, Lord.' Dr. Scroggie said to the one he was counselling that that was a contradiction in three words: you cannot say 'Lord' and at the same time say 'not so'! So he asked that troubled Christian to face those three words. He gave her a pencil and said, 'You must strike out either "not so" or "Lord",' and he left. He came back some few minutes later, to find her with her head bowed and her Bible open; and as he looked at the Bible he saw that the pencil had been drawn through the words 'not so'!

Is there any area in your life or mine in which the Lordship of Jesus Christ is not wanted? Disturbance – the most disturbing person you could ever meet is Christ. Disorder; disturbance; and we find, finally and unbelievably –

DISMISSAL BY THE COMMUNITY TO WHICH CHRIST CAME. 'The whole multitude ... besought him to depart from them.' We find here *a tragedy that was inexcusable.* Let us grasp it in the sheer bluntness of it: they told Jesus Christ to get out. They did; and I wouldn't be surprised if there are some Christians saying to Jesus Christ, the Lord whose interference in your life you're afraid, of, 'Get out! I don't mind thinking of you as the Saviour from the sins that I'm ashamed of: but I'm not going to have you running my life. Get out!'

And He got out! But who was this One they were dismissing? They besought Him...' Who is the 'Him'? He is Jesus, the Son of God, the Saviour of the world. They didn't want Him! What a staggering, what a shameful fact; but it was true!

Some years ago I heard Bishop Taylor Smith preaching at Keswick. To us who were young at the time, he was almost a legendary figure; he was *the* Bishop. Portly, gracious, and oh so faithful if he got you alone! That godly, saintly man knew something of the kind of challenge that the convention could hold, and one year – not in the tent, I believe, but in St. John's or Crosthwaite church – Bishop Taylor Smith felt impelled to preach on the parable of the prodigal son, and particularly on the words concerning the elder brother, 'he was angry, and would not go in.' He spoke of how the very challenge of the grace of God, and the message of the Word of God, could produce a reaction of anger and resentment; and that we could get so angry that we would exclude ourselves from all that God was waiting to give. It proved to be God's word to at least one man in the church. Angry! I wonder if that's the kind of reaction that some of us have found beginning to take control of our thinking. We find ourselves getting a bit cross, and even a bit mad at the preacher!

The tragedy that was inexcusable. 'They besought Him to depart.' These people said to Jesus Christ, 'Get out!' And He went. But there's one ray of hope; we mustn't leave out just one factor in the situation: *the testimony that was inescapable.* Because although Jesus went, this man whom He had healed remained; and the question that must always arise in our minds is, did Jesus come back again? The witness of the Scripture is that He did; and I think Jesus Christ left that man behind in order that he might prepare the way for Him to come. This man went all over Decapolis telling the people what Christ had done for him. His transformed life was such a testimony that when later on we read in Matt. 15 of Christ coming back again, after having gone to Tyre and Sidon, and coming down through the coast of Decapolis, we find that 'great multitudes came'. And, after they had seen all that Christ had been able to do when they welcomed Him, they glorified the God of Israel.

It may be that some of us will want to reject the sovereignty of Christ from our experience. I hope and pray that somebody, living maybe in your home – a child of yours, a husband or a wife; somebody in your church, somebody in your street, some relative will bear such a testimony that you will be compelled to realise that the only right attitude to Jesus is to welcome Him for all that He is. Maybe you are in grave danger of doing exactly what these people did. You don't mind Christ dealing with your helplessness; you want to be rid of these things that hurt you and that hurt others; you want to be rid of the discomfort of it all. But if Jesus Christ is going to start interfering with the whole pattern of your life, if Jesus Christ is going to insist that you cannot be the same as the world, if you find that it's going to affect you, yes, even your pocket, then your attitude is, Get out!

But remember, please, who it is you're dismissing. You're telling Jesus Christ, the Son of God, the Lord of glory, to get out of your life. That is what you are doing. And the supreme tragedy of your life will be that, if you persist in that, He will do as you wish. He will get out. Do you really want Him to go? Or do you want to welcome Him, and give Him His way in your life in every department? How simple it is, isn't it? It's the old, old lesson that we found so difficult to learn when we were bairns at home, and our fathers and mothers used to say to us, 'When will you learn to do as you're told?' When will you? But it affects the whole of life; and when you and I bring the whole of life and put it at the disposal of Jesus Christ, then the whole of our life is going to be covered by the whole of our Saviour. His adequacy and His authority; and blessed be His name, His availability to meet every situation at any moment of any time.

10

The greatest thing Jesus ever said

'God so loved the world, that he gave his only begotten Son, that whosoever believeth in him should not perish, but have everlasting life' (John 3. 16).

THIS VERSE HAS been rightly called the greatest text in the Bible; indeed the truths contained in it are so great that no preacher attempts the task of preaching on it lightly. In some ways it is so familiar that every hearer of sermons might wonder what can be said upon it that has not been said a hundred times before. Surely it must be the most preached-on text in the whole Bible, and yet no other verse says so much, so clearly and so concisely as this text, and so we cannot leave it out in our series on the life of Jesus Christ. There are three things I am sure that any preacher would want to say about this text. The first is that it speaks of –

THE GREATEST LOVE THAT A MAN CAN EVER KNOW. 'God so loved the world,' and that greatest love is of course the love of God. Bishop Taylor Smith used to say that the heart of the Christian message lies in three short sentences: 'God is,' 'God is love,' 'God loves you.' Surely there can be no greater tragedy in life than for a person to be unloved, and because they are unloved to feel they are unwanted. I remember hearing over the radio on Sunday morning a minister from Sydney, Australia, recalling how a girl had been brought to his church. She had been found in a park running away from shadows that did not exist. She was high on drugs, and communication was almost impossible. She was taken to hospital, but the only word that they could get out of her was one word written on a bit of paper, and the word was 'lonely'. Some of us who have been blessed in our lives with love on the human level may scarcely realise what it means to be unloved and unwanted. But these words of Jesus Christ assure us that *no one* is unloved by God, and no one is therefore unwanted.

Someone has said so very truly that the greatest need in every life is 'to have someone to love, and to have someone to be loved by'. Think for a moment of *the importance that love gives to a life*. If something is loved, then that thing whatever it may be becomes important. If a person is loved, then that person whoever they may be becomes important; and this is what lies at the heart of the message of Jesus Christ. The message that comes to anyone, that comes to everyone, is the message that says 'you are important', 'you matter', 'you matter enormously to God'. Sometimes in our lives we speak of losing something that we describe as being 'of great sentimental value'. The value of such a possession to us cannot be estimated in terms of money; we could get its value in money to replace it if it was stolen or lost, but that would not be the same thing. And what is true of things and possessions is also true of people. Just because God loves you, you matter! You are important. It may be that others do not set the same value upon you, but God does, and you matter to Him as much as anyone else. No one can ever say they are unloved. No one can ever say they are unwanted.

And so we pause to assess the value which the love of God sets upon a human life. I remember hearing of a traveller crossing a bridge between Cannes and Nice. There was a bunch of flowers on the parapet of this high bridge, and on asking why it was there, the traveller was told that a short while previously a wealthy girl in a sports car had drawn up and had taken her dog in her arms and had leapt over the parapet of the bridge to her death. She had left a note in her car which said, 'Nobody loves me but my dog. There is no peace.' What a pity that girl did not know that she *was* loved, and that she *was* wanted.

But not only do we realise the importance love gives to a life, but *the difference that love makes to a life*. Not only does love give a new value, but it brings a new vision – the vision of giving pleasure to another, of rendering service to another, and by accepting the demands that both of these will make. The result is that a new sense of purpose, a new meaning comes into life, a new world opens out before me. The world of another life to consider, to plan for, to sacrifice for, for I matter to that other person and I find that that other person matters to me. So adjustments will be made in my appearance, adjustments will be made in my time-table to find time for that other, to make room for the wishes and the interests of that other. This is surely what the Bible is getting at when it tells us that for God's pleasure 'all things are, and were created'. Man has been created to *give* pleasure to God and to *find* pleasure in giving pleasure to Him. The shorter catechism in answering the question, 'What is the chief end of man?' answers, 'To glorify God and to enjoy Him forever.' All this brings a new meaningfulness into living; it gives a sense of purpose to life when we discover that in Jesus Christ and the message of the good news that He brought, we find the greatest love we can every know. 'God so loved the world.' But this greatest text of the Bible goes on to speak of –

THE GREATEST GIFT A MAN CAN EVER HAVE. 'God so loved the world *that He gave* His only begotten Son.' The gift of

God's love is the gift of Christ Himself; and what greater gift could anyone have than that! What preacher would want to leave that out of his message? But let us think, first, of *the desire love has in giving*: and love's desire is usually a combination of two things. Love will want to give in order to meet a need. A mother planning to give to a child may think long and hard as to what that child needs – a new pair of shoes, a new dress, a new suit of clothes. But love may also plan just to thrill a heart: the gift to a sweetheart is designed to bring and give delight and pleasure. So love will give either what we need or what we would like, and in the case of the love of God, surely that desire will be guided by a wisdom that is perfect and will make no mistakes. God's love and God's wisdom know what we need, and that will also check carefully what we want, lest what we want should not be wise or right. God's love is therefore a giving love. How we need to believe this, for so many people believe the very opposite. They seem to think that God is a thief: that He is out to spoil our fun, to impoverish our lives, and that if we respond to the love of God it will mean giving up so much. I don't think, really, it means giving up anything except sin, which God's love and wisdom know could never give us happiness anyway! What man is faced with in the giving of the love of God, is not so much a matter of giving up but of giving *in* to this love which offers us so much in Christ. After all, is this not what our Lord Himself spoke about in John 10. 10? There we have those tremendous words of His, 'The thief cometh ... to steal, and to kill, and to destroy; I am come that they might have life, and that they might have it more abundantly.' Christ is the gift of the love of God. He was given for us on the cross to die for our sins; He is given *to* us by His Spirit to dwell in our lives, to lift the guilt of my sin, and to break the chains of my sin. This is the desire that love has in giving – always to enrich, never to impoverish.

But then, when we think of the giving of love, we realise also *the demand love meets in giving*. Everyone who gives knows that every gift has a price, the payment of which is sometimes costly either in terms of money that has to be paid, or time and skill and trouble that has to be taken. And if this is true of human giving, it is also true of the giving of the love of God. There was and is a demand that that love has to meet in giving. The Christ who is given to me by the Holy Spirit was first of all given for me on the cross. How beautifully and exquisitely the children's hymn puts this –

> There is a green hill far away,
>   Without a city wall,
> Where the dear Lord was crucified,
>   Who died to save us all.
>
> There was no other good enough
>   To pay the price of sin;
> He only could unlock the gate
>   Of heaven, and let us in.
>
> We may not know, we cannot tell
>   What pains He had to bear;
> But we believe it was for us
>   He hung and suffered there.

The Bible says that we were redeemed 'not with corruptible things, as silver and gold . . . but with the precious blood of Christ.' I remember hearing Dr. Charles Stern tell of an incident during the war when he served as a chaplain. Night time had come, and the soldiers were in an exposed and dangerous part of the front. The padre's companion was the doctor. The doctor had a warm coat, but the padre had none – maybe he had already given his to someone else. The night was going to be cold, and the doctor was determined that the padre should have his coat to keep him warm, and the padre was equally determined that he would not. After a protracted argument they lay down to sleep, but just before the

padre fell asleep he suddenly felt the coat being laid upon
him. Dr. Stern's comment was, 'the doctor took the cold and
I took the coat!' And so, in a mystery beyond all human
understanding – and we should not be surprised to find it so
– Christ took the guilt of our sin. He paid the price, if you
like, for the forgiveness of our sins, in the mystery of His
death upon the cross. The *dying* of Christ was in some deep,
unfathomable way a *doing* by God, a dealing with the guilt
of the sin on mankind: and here was the demand that love
had to meet.

We have considered the greatest love we can ever know,
the greatest gift we can ever have. But our verse goes on to
say that 'God so loved the world that He gave His only
begotten Son *that whosoever believeth in him* should not
perish, but have everlasting life.' And so we face, finally –

THE GREATEST CHOICE A MAN CAN EVER MAKE. For after all,
when a gift is offered we have to choose whether or not we
are prepared to receive it. Life is full of choices, and we
cannot grumble at this: it would be a strange way of life if
we were not free to choose, and although there may be many
influences affecting our choice, in the final analysis the
choice is mine and choose I must. I have to choose what I
will do with my time, with my money, with my life, and with
my Lord. And when I face the choice concerning what I am
to do with Christ, surely that is the greatest choice that I can
ever make. Partly because it deals with the greatest person in
my life, and also because it will have the greatest effect in my
life.

I want to note, first, *the respect that God shows for us* in
leaving the choice finally to ourselves. God is respecting, as
respect He must, the integrity of our human personality.
The choice is ours, let us face that. The Scripture reads, 'that
whosoever believeth in Him should not perish'. God will do
everything possible to encourage us to make the right choice.
We can see how others have made this choice. We can hear

through the preaching of God's Word that the choice is there to be made. We can know in our own lives the sense of pressure as God through His Holy Spirit urges us to make the right choice; but in the final analysis, the choice is ours. It is open to anyone and everyone: the words make this plain, 'that whosoever believeth in him...' It is always a strange thing to me that some people resent the fact that they have to decide about Jesus Christ, when they accept that they are free to decide about almost everything else in life! They decide, don't they, about the person they are going to marry, the dress they are going to wear, the car they are going to buy. What is wrong, then, with having to choose either to accept or reject Jesus Christ? God continually confronts His people with the need to choose. Do you remember the tremendous words of Joshua long ago to the people of God, 'Choose you this day whom ye will serve'? Becoming a Christian is not a matter of chance; it is a matter of choice! Some people might argue, 'But what about the sovereignty of God, what about election, what about predestination?' As I read the Scriptures, the sovereignty of God is not concerned with the people who are to be saved, but with the *person through whom* alone any man can and must be saved. That person is Christ, we are 'chosen in Him'. The sovereignty of God is also concerned with the condition of faith in that person to be fulfilled if we are to be saved. The sovereignty of God and His elective purpose has also to do with *the purposes for which* men are saved. We are 'elect unto obedience'. But 'whosoever' and 'if any man' occur too often in the New Testament to indicate that man does not choose. Choose he must, and choose he can! Ah, but somebody says, How can someone who is spiritually 'dead in sin' choose? the answer of course is that although man may be spiritually dead, man is not morally irresponsible; he still is a moral being with the power to choose, and choose he must!

The respect God shows for us; and lastly, I note *the re-*

sponse God seeks from us: 'That whosoever believeth in him should not perish, but have everlasting life.' I note the simplicity of the response that God seeks from us; the simplicity and the necessity of the faith with which we can and must respond. Everything is available for us in Christ, just as everything is available for a sick man in a surgeon. All that is needed is for the sinner to put his faith in the Saviour, just as a sick man must put his faith in the surgeon. When that happens, all the resources of the surgeon's skill are available for the sick man, and all the resources of the grace of God in the Saviour are available for the sinner.

The greatest choice we can ever make. And it is that, when we think how much there is to gain – 'everlasting life', a new quality of life that begins on earth and lasts for ever; and when we think how much there is to lose now and hereafter, all this lies beneath the word 'perish'. We are called upon to put our confidence and trust in Jesus Christ, knowing Him to be the Saviour He is; to trust Him in His grace, His wisdom, and to take Him in all the wonder of His living presence to dwell in our hearts by His Holy Spirit.

Some years ago in a mental hospital some words were found scribbled on the wall written by a patient, a song that became well-known through the singing of George Beverly Shea; and I close with these, as they seem to sum up all that we have been thinking about in these words of Jesus Christ –

> Could we with ink the ocean fill,
>   And were the skies of parchment made;
> Were every stalk of grass a quill,
>   And every man a scribe by trade:
>
> To write the love of God above
>   Would drain the ocean dry;
> Nor could the scroll contain the whole,
>   Though stretched from sky to sky.

> Oh, love of God, how rich and pure,
>   How measureless and strong:
> It shall for evermore endure
>   The saints' and angels' song.

The greatest love we can ever know. The greatest gift we can
ever have. The greatest choice we can ever make!

One of my earliest memories of the great Keswick Convention was hearing the late Dr. W. Y. Fullerton speaking in
the big tent. It was the last time he spoke, for before the next
convention he had gone to be with his Lord. He was looking
back over a long life in which he had proved the faithfulness
of his God, and his face glowed as he bore his testimony to
his Lord. He recalled how in his teens he had become a
Christian, and how he had heard somebody speak on the
words, 'The gift of God is eternal life through Jesus Christ',
and the speaker commenting on these words said something
quite simple: he said, 'A gift becomes yours when you take
it.' Dr. Fullerton said that that day he took the gift of God in
Jesus Christ, and his comment was, 'It was mine because I
took it.' As we come to the end of this tremendous theme of
this the greatest text in the Bible each of us must face the
fact that God did so love the world that He did give His only
begotten Son, and that faces us with the question: the gift is
there, but is it mine? Have I taken it; or rather, have I taken
Him? If I have, then I will know in a deep and real way
something of what we have been thinking about in this the
greatest text in the Bible, the greatest thing that Jesus ever
said, where we have been facing he greatest love we can
ever know, the greatest gift we can ever have, and the greatest choice we can ever make. Have you accepted that gift? Is
Jesus Christ yours?

11

Christ, Lord of the sabbath day

'The sabbath was made for man, and not man for the sabbath; therefore the Son of man is Lord also of the sabbath' (Mark 2. 27–28).

FEW SUBJECTS ARE surrounded with more controversy and argument than the way in which Christians and others should, or should not observe the sabbath day. Few Scriptures are more frequently misquoted than the verses we have taken as our text for our study on 'Christ ... Lord of the sabbath day'. Most of those who quote this particular reference in Scripture quote only v. 27, and leave out the second verse with its much more demanding statement.

When asked to address a meeting of the Lord's Day Observance Society, and with a desire to be positive rather than negative, I felt that a helpful way to approach the subject might be to ask and answer the question, 'How did the Lord of the day observe the day Himself?' To guide my thoughts I decided to check up on every reference that I could find in the Gospels which could shed some light upon this question. I found myself then asking three questions to find an answer

to my basic question, how did the Lord of the day observe
the day? The first question I asked myself was –

WHERE DID THE LORD OF THE DAY GO ON THE SABBATH DAY?
I discovered that He is named as being found in three
different kinds of places. I find that He went to *the services
of the synagogue* on the Lord's day. Luke 4. 16 tells us that
'He went into the synagogue on the sabbath day, as His
custom was.' This would surely be a habit formed and a
practice observed that found Him every sabbath day in the
house of God in the place of worship. And one would not be
far off the mark if one assumed that some of the services
might not be too inspiring, but He was there! I like to think
that this habit was formed in His early years, and that for
this He had to thank His earthly parents. Habits formed in
childhood are not too easily or readily broken. I remember
hearing of an old lady who was asked why she went to
church every Sunday. Her reply was, 'I like to let people
know which side I am on.' Surely we would do well to follow
the example of our Lord in the forming and the keeping of
this habit. Although in fairness I think we have to admit
that the last thing that could be said about some church
services is that God is worshipped! Maybe from those
churches it might be better to stay away, and find a church
where God is worshipped in spirit and in truth.

I find also that He went to *the houses of the people* on the
sabbath day. In Luke 14. 1–6 we are told that 'He went into
the house of one of the chief Pharisees to eat bread on the
sabbath day.' No doubt He had been invited, and had gladly
accepted the invitation. Was it after the services in the synagogue? We are not told. But that was where He went on
that sabbath day. This was something that seemed acceptable to Him. No doubt, and we shall touch on this later, it
was because of the opportunity this visit would give Him to
put such an occasion to good use, of making it serve a much
deeper purpose than existed in the minds of those who had

invited Him. Is there a hint here for us that the Lord of the day might want to use our homes, or through us to use the homes of some friends, to fulfil some divine and deeper purpose? Sometimes we are in danger of thinking that God's house is the only house to be used on the Lord's day, but the example of our Lord would indicate otherwise. Our homes, the homes of our friends, are to be used for deeper and divine purposes that maybe have as yet never entered our thinking!

I find Him also going where *the needs of the world* could be found and seen. In John 5. 1 we find Him at the pool of Bethesda, where we are told 'there lay a great multitude of impotent folk', and in v. 9 we are told that that day was the sabbath. In John 9. 1 we find Him out walking along the road, and there He comes across a man blind from birth; and again in v. 14 we are told that it was the sabbath day. In other words, the sabbath day was a day when Jesus seems to have gone out of His way to make contact with people who were in need, to seek them out where they would be found. In Mark 2. 23 we read of Him taking His disciples with Himself for a walk through the cornfields on the sabbath day. I suppose that one of the obvious reasons for this was that on that day some people would be more accessible and available than on a weekday, when everyone would be preoccupied with their daily work. Do we need to face the challenge of this, the implications of this in our own self-centred programming of even our sabbath days? Christ did not go only to the house of God, not just to the homes of people, but He went where the needs of men could be seen and met.

We might do well to pause and ask ourselves whether the places where we go on the Lord's day bear any resemblance to the places where He went on that day. That was my first question, 'Where did He go on the Lord's day?'

The second question I found myself asking was –

WHAT DID THE LORD OF THE DAY DO ON THE SABBATH DAY?

And again I have tried to find out what the Gospels have to tell us about this aspect of His life and teaching. When I think of Him going to the services of the synagogue I realise that part of the time there would be spent in *hearing the Word of God*, listening to what the Word of God in the Old Testament had to say of God's will for men. This was and is surely the very heart of true worship. We live in a day when it is fashionable in some ecclesiastical quarters to denigrate the place of the Word of God in worship, and in others to exaggerate it. In some services ten minutes is regarded as the ideal of a sermon; in others not less than forty-five minutes will suffice! In Christ's own definition of worship He made it plain that 'they that worship . . . must worship in spirit and in truth.' Surely that means that if in worship we are to give to our God His worth in our lives, then we must not only know Him in truth but also be truly and rightly related to Him. If the preaching of the Word of God is presented in such a way that in both matter and in manner it is acceptable to God and digestible by man, then we have some hope that the worship which will result from such a presentation of the truth of God will enable true worship to be offered. I believe that the highest point of worship in any service should come, and will come, at the end of the preaching of the Word of God, when men are brought to know Him better and to respond more completely to His word and will. I question if there is any greater need in the life of the Church in our land than to assess exactly what place the Word of God is to have in the services of the Church of Jesus Christ. The ten-minute sermonette is normally ludicrously inadequate, although from some preachers it will be ten minutes too long! Forty-five minutes from a few preachers will prove to be an unforgettable experience, but from the majority of preachers, an unforgivable one!

What else did He do on the sabbath day? I find Him not only hearing the Word of God, but also *sharing the truth of God*. We find Him doing this formally in the synagogue as preacher, but also informally in the homes of the people. In that home of the Pharisee, watch how He guided the conversation round to talk frankly about the deeper things of the faith, until He was able to confront those present with God's invitation to a greater feast at a table where there would always be room for more to find their place! I sometimes wonder if we have blundered badly in leaving all the talking about our faith to what is said in our churches and by our preachers. I often wonder if the more effective line would be if ordinary people had the courage to share their faith with their friends in the informality of their homes. One thing I do know, and that is that the churches which are growing today are the churches where that kind of sharing is going on. Have we ever caught the vision of letting the Lord use our homes as well as our churches? No doubt there are problems, and there are those seekers of position who would have a harmful influence and would tend to set up little churches in their homes; but in principle, the strategy is basically a sound one and should be explored. It is good that we should invite friends to come to our churches, and how few of us ever do it; but what about inviting them as well to our homes, and sharing the truth of God with them when the opportunity to do so presents itself as, in time, it will most surely do.

Hearing the Word of God, sharing the truth of God, and one more thing seems to have occupied His mind and His time: I call that *meeting the needs of men*. Not just their spiritual needs, although these were always there, but other needs as well, physical or emotional. Here it is a blind man receiving his sight on the sabbath day. Here it is a crippled woman being made straight on the sabbath day. Here it is a man with the dropsy being healed on the sabbath day. Here it is a man with a withered hand, being restored on the sabbath day. Here it is a group of discouraged disciples being encouraged on the sabbath day. None of these needs were superficial, but deep basic and urgent needs, many of them no doubt having deep spiritual undertones. The point is that we find our Lord seeking such people out on the sabbath day. He went where they were. He did not wait for them to come to Him. And having found them, He brought to bear upon them in their need the full resources of the love, grace and power of God. Some of the encounters did take place in the synagogue, and it may be that some of the greatest needs are still to be found in the lives of those who gather to worship in the house of God. But not all were found there. Do we need to grasp this fact, that the Lord seems to have made good use of the whole day, the whole time. So often we think in terms of our attendance at church, where we sit on our bottoms and wait for others to come to us, while all the time, like our Lord, we should be on our feet going to where they are to be found.

So far we have asked two questions and have tried to answer them. Here is our third and last question –

WHAT DID THE LORD OF THE DAY SAY ABOUT THE DAY? And here we come back to the two verses we chose as our text: 'The sabbath was made for man, and not man for the sabbath; therefore the Son of man is Lord also of the sabbath day.' There are three things that I think we can find in what the Lord had to say about the sabbath day.

He speaks of *the control that day must enjoy* – 'The Son of man is Lord also of the sabbath day.' How seldom is this verse ever referred to! It surely implies that in some very special way the Lord wants us to set aside for that one day those matters that concern us on all the other days, and instead find out and become occupied with the things that are peculiarly of concern to Him. Someone once said that God demands a tenth of our money and a seventh of our time; an apt saying with a very considerable measure of truth in it! It certainly means that this day comes in a very special way under His authority. He will have the planning of it, and not ourselves. And in the light of all that we have been talking about there is nothing negative about this, but rather something wonderfully positive. The Lord's day should be the richest and the loveliest day of the whole week. It ought to be in many ways the fullest and the most creative day of all the seven days of the week. I still believe that the fourth commandment, like all the other nine of the ten commandments, is binding on men. I believe too, that in keeping the day 'holy' we are meant to keep it as a day apart, a separate special day, separated from certain things and separated for certain other things.

He speaks, too, of *the concern the day should express.* He says, 'It was made for man' for man in the totality of his personality. Most of the other needs of man can be met on all the other six days of the week, but on this special day some special needs are to be met, needs that when met will affect every other part of man's life for his good. The provision of this one day in seven is an expression not just of the law of God, but of the love of God. There is truth in the old saying that 'a sabbath well spent brings a week of content'. Man cannot be truly and fully happy unless living in a right relationship with his Creator God. This one day in seven is a golden opportunity to maintain that relationship in good order, not simply for man individually, but in the fellowship and company of others for mutual enrichment and encouragement, and to endeavour to bring others into that right relationship as well.

There is one other aspect to note, and that centres around *the conflict the day will evoke* when thus observed. Very often when our Lord ran into trouble with His enemies it was as a direct result of what He had done or said on the sabbath day. As far as He was concerned He had observed the day in complete harmony with the Father's will; but that did not always fit in with the ideas of others. But as we listen to our Lord's words we can sense that He was not willing to give way one inch – 'Ought not this woman whom Satan hath bound be loosed on the sabbath day?' 'Is it not lawful to do well on the sabbath day?' The guiding principle was to act on that day in accordance with what would be pleasing to the Father, and that is the guiding principle still.

What a wonderful day the Lord's day is obviously meant to be. It is meant to be a day that is positive, creative, attractive, and productive of man's highest good and happiness. Surely of this day in a very special way we can say with the Psalmist, 'This is the day that the Lord hath made, therefore we will rejoice and be glad in it.' And as we rejoice in this day and handle it, we will find that not only do we rejoice in it, but others will rejoice with us as well!

12

Christ's portrait of a Christian

'Blessed are the poor in spirit ... they that mourn ... the meek ... they which do hunger and thirst after righteousness ... the merciful ... the pure in heart ... the persecuted ...' (Matthew 5. 1–12).

I WANT TO consider the question, Are we recognisable Christians? In Acts 11. 26 we read that 'the disciples were called Christians first in Antioch.' They did not call themselves Christians. You and I do that. They were called Christians by others, who recognised them to be such. So I want us to consider this vital question, Are you, am I, recognisable Christians? And in order to do that, I want to turn to the opening verses of Matt. 5, which I venture to call 'Christ's portrait of a Christian'. We have Paul's portrait of a Christian in 1 Cor. 13; we have another in the Galatian letter. But I wonder if this is really a portrait of what Christ means us to be?

Christ's portrait of a Christian! I wonder what we shall find there? Surprisingly it is framed in radiant splendour! For Christ says that basically, and whichever way you look at the Christian life, it is a radiant and splendid thing;

radiant with joy and happiness and goodness. For of everything that He has to say here, He says that the man is 'blessed',
or happy, radiant, joyous! I do not know how much radiant
Christianity there is today. We see a lot of dowdy and dull
Christianity, but very little radiant Christian living. What
do we find there as our great Master takes the pigments and
portrays what He conceives to be the Christian?

We find the most extraordinary things here. In v. 3 we
find, first of all, *poverty*. Strange portrait, this! Blessed are
the poor in spirit; for theirs is the Kingdom of Heaven.' Yes,
you will find poverty in the portrait. Here is the Christian's
estimate of himself. He is poor in his own eyes. There is no
hint of satisfaction, no indication anywhere of self-
sufficiency, no smugness, no sense of superiority; but rather,
a recognition of his own utter bankruptcy and poverty. He
uses the language of St. Paul, 'I know that in me . . . dwelleth
no good thing . . . I count not myself to have apprehended.'
Poverty. A strange picture, isn't it? But let us remember that
this is a picture drawn by the Master's own hand; and the
first thing that He etches in is poverty – but a poverty that
leads on to possession. For having faced his own poverty, the
Christian has found a possession in the Kingdom of heaven;
his right to enter that Kingdom, to enjoy it, to know something of the authority of its rule and the adequacy of is
resources. If you and I measure ourselves up against the
portrait that our Lord has painted here, that is the first thing
that we shall find – poverty. That is our estimate of ourselves. We are poor.

The second thing that we find – strange picture, this – we
find *burdens* here. 'Blessed are they that mourn: for they
shall be comforted.' The Christian life as our Lord conceives
it, is a life marked by sorrow, by concern. A Christian is
someone who cares, who cares deeply; someone who grieves.
His mind is marked by an extreme sensitiveness, an openness
of heart and mind, not just to his own need, but to the need
of his fellows; to the need of his God. Whether that need be

sin, or sorrow, or suffering, the Christian gets under the burden of it, and he cares. Yet with his concern he has found consolation and comfort; consolation in the knowledge that something is being done, has been done, will be done — either that pardon can be found, or has been found; either that prayer has been offered, and therefore God will work, or that God's purposes are being fulfilled. When you and I look into the portrait of the Christian as penned by Christ, we find that there are burdens there.

Poverty, burdens; and then, strangely, *silence.* 'Blessed are the meek; for they shall inherit the earth.' Humility has indeed been defined as the 'silence of the soul before God'. Meekness and humility have strangely little to say whenever they are facing the strains and tensions of human relationships; humility and meekness have nothing to say about injury received. They accept injury without resentment and are silent about it. They have nothing to add to praise that has been given; indeed, meekness and humility will not accept praise. There is an extraordinary silence about itself, its injuries and its achievements. Meekness and humility are not talkative about themselves or anything concerning themselves. Not only silence about things that can be said and done in facing human relationships, but in fulfilling divine requirements. Whatever the will of God might be for the soul, meekness fulfils it and obeys it, content that it is the will of God. But the extraordinary thing is that this very silence, this very meekness, is something which inherits the earth; which brings that silent life into spheres of influence, of responsibility, literally all over the earth, with an ever widening circle of life to which it is bound. I wonder how much of the earth we have inherited? Is there a sphere of influence, of responsibility, that is ours because we are meek enough to pray? We will certainly get no popularity from praying; we will get no applause for it, and pride will find nothing on which to feed in prayer. But we will inherit that part of the earth for which you pray; a sphere of influence and responsibility will become yours, the end of which only eternity will reveal. The meek Christian has a wonderful circle of influence, with people and things that he knows, and that in a strange way have become his own peculiar possession.

Burdens, poverty, silence. You will find *desire* also: 'Blessed are they which do hunger and thirst after righteousness: for they shall be filled.' Desire that will take a man to his knees in secret; that will take him to pray in fellowship with others. For desire and prayer have been linked by his Lord, and well he will pray about it. He will desire intensely that God's way with his own life may be fulfilled; that God's work in the world may be carried out; and in the answering of those prayers his desires will be met, either in some new discovery of God, or in watching some doing by God. Yes, as our Lord portrays the Christian, He portrays him on his knees. You will find desire there.

Then, as our Lord fills in the details – strange picture this, isn't it? – you will find *kindness* there. 'Blessed are the merciful: for they shall obtain mercy.' Sheer kindness, understanding kindness, sympathy; nothing of roughness or rudeness, nothing harsh; a gentleness of touch, a patience of attitude, a kindness in tone, which will in its turn receive from men a response of gratitude and kindliness. If it is true anywhere it is true here, that 'what measure ye mete to others, it shall be measured to you again'.

You will find more: you will find *reality* here. 'Blessed are the pure in heart: for they shall see God.' The pure in heart – there is no hypocrisy here, no hidden corners of treasured and deliberate insincerity, but instead an honesty, a frankness, an openness towards God, of intention, of resolve, if not of success and achievement. There is no false element, no insincerity, nothing that is not genuine or real. One of the soldiers of Napoleon was wounded, and as the surgeons probed for a bullet that was lodged near his heart, the man in his pain, as they probed deeper and still deeper, said, 'An-

other inch, and you'll find the Emperor!' The deeper you go
into the Christian, the truer he is. Who was it said of
Fred Mitchell, 'You never caught Fred Mitchell off his
guard, because he had no need to be on it'? 'Blessed are the
pure in heart: for they shall see God.' Reality in our every
attitude to God, and reality in our experience of God.

Yes, you will find poverty there, burdens, silence, desire,
kindness, reality. And you will find *serenity* there. 'Blessed
are the peacemakers: for they shall be called the children of
God.' Serenity – for how can one make peace, who knows it
not? Peace has been defined as the possession of adequate
resources. Peace before the accuser; peace before the di-
lemmas of life: peace through the adequacy of the resources
of grace that we have discovered, and now long to share. A
serenity, a quietness, a peace, in the presence of which men
find rest, or seek it; in the presence of which quarrels die,
and discords die away: a life explainable only in terms of a
relationship to God, and marked by a likeness to Him.
'Godly'. Called that by others. What are you called? What
do people call you? Do they call you difficult? Do they call
you proud? Do they call you critical? Do they call you unre-
liable? Do they call you touchy? What do they call you?
'Blessed are the peacemakers, for they shall be called the
children of God.'

There is one more thing you will find. You will find
wounds there. 'Blessed are they which are persecuted for
righteousness' sake: for theirs is the kingdom of heaven.'
Blessed are ye, when men shall revile you, and persecute you,
and shall say all manner of evil against you falsely, for my
sake. Rejoice, and be exceeding glad . . .' You will find
wounds there. Wounded by the tongues of men, wounded by
the deeds of men, unjustly, falsely: they have hurt; deliberately they said it; and the wound bleeds and does not heal.

Hast thou no wound? Yet I was wounded by the archers;
Spent, leaned me against a tree to die,

And rent by ravening wolves that compassed me, I swooned;
Hast thou no wound?

Hast thou no scar? No hidden scar on foot or side, or hand?
I hear thee sung as mighty in the land;
I hear them hail thy bright, ascendant star;
Hast thou no scar?

No wound, no scar? Yet as the Master shall the servant be,
And pierced are the feet that follow me.
But thine are whole. Can he have followed far
Who has no wound, no scar?

You will find wounds there!

Christ's portrait of the Christian. Poverty, burdens,
silence, desire, kindness, reality, serenity, wounds. Christ's
portrait of the Christian? No: Christ's portrait of *you*, and
me! Do we recognise it; or have we just been playing at
being Christians? What the world needs is Jesus; just a
glimpse of Him. They do not want to listen, they want to
look; and as they look at you, and as they look at me, they
just do not recognise us. And yet we read, 'the disciples were
called Christians first at Antioch'.

I want us to ask ourselves, 'Are we recognisable Christians?' And if we are not recognisable Christians, then for
God's sake let us confess our sin. Is this what is wrong with
the Church? Is this what is holding up revival? It is just that
we Christians are playing at the business; getting a kick out
of it, but not being it. I wonder if I lived with you, I wonder
if you were a member of my church, I wonder if I worked
alongside you, I wonder if I were one of your children, I
wonder if I were the neighbour living next door, if I had in
my hand Christ's portrait of a Christian, and then I looked
at you, I wonder if I should recognise it?

Orthodox, converted, keen, zealous, but not recognisable.
And that is what is wrong. Why not let us take the portrait?

We have carried it in our Bibles for years, but we have never really looked at it – not really. Then let us ask Christ, in His mercy, as He indwells us by His Spirit, to do in us what He has done there; and that is, portray the true Christians that we are meant to be, so that we shall not need to call ourselves Christians any more, because we shall be *called* Christians, recognised as Christians. Then maybe in God's mercy, others, as they recognise and see something of what a Christian life really is, will begin to see the radiance of it and the joy and the wonder and the glory of it, and long to find the same life for themselves.

13

How a Christian rises from his knees

'The kingdom ... the power ... the glory ...' (Matthew 6. 13).

I WANT TO consider some very familiar words. And yet right away when I mention these words, we face a problem. They come in the Sermon on the Mount, the final phrases of what we call 'The Lord's Prayer', which is of course, the pattern prayer which Jesus gave to His disciples. We face a problem, because if your Bible is an RSV or an NEB you will not find the words there that are in the Authorised Version. They have been transferred to the margin, with the comment, 'Other authorities, some ancient, add them.' The words, are, of course, 'For Thine is the kingdom, and the power, and the glory, for ever.'

There would seem to be two reasons for their omission from the RSV and the NEB. One is that in St. Luke's version of the Lord's prayer, we do not find them. I think, however, it is important to note that the occasion when our Lord was giving the prayer, as recorded in Luke's Gospel, was a different one, and I am sure our Lord must have repeated Himself again and again in His teaching in different places; and I don't think we can assume that in speaking on separate occasions He necessarily spoke precisely the same words. What preacher or teacher ever does? The other reason, which is possibly a more serious one, as explained in the margin of the RSV and the NEB, is that while some ancient manuscripts include the words, some scholars maintain that the oldest that we have, omit them. But that still leaves open another possibility, that one day we shall find a still older manuscript which does include them! I like to think that these words *were* spoken by our blessed Lord. To me they seem to round off so perfectly the family prayer, with this note of doxology and praise. Whatever we may think about the words themselves, we need have no uncertainty about the truths enshrined in them. And it is with these truths that I want to be concerned now: 'Thine is the kingdom . . . and the power . . . and the glory, for ever.'

I wonder if some of us hope that some day, somehow or other we will discover the secret of living the Christian life as it ought to be lived; that we will come across some formula that will ensure that the clouds will roll away and all will be sunshine. I want to offer to you not a formula, nor an experience, but to set out three principles upon which the Christian life must surely be lived, if it is to be lived adequately and worthily. The principles are in these words, if we can really say them: 'Thine is the kingdom, and the power, and the glory, for ever.' The first affirmation these words contain is that the Christian is to live a life –

CONTROLLED BY THE WILL OF GOD. 'Thine is the kingdom.' Now while I recognise that this affirmation has implications that cover the whole canvas of history, indeed of the universe, the implications of it include us! Here we face again this simple truth, that the hallmark of a valid Christian life lies in its obedience to the will of God. Our Lord made it plain: 'Ye are my friends, *if* ye do whatsoever I command you.' 'He that hath my commandments, and keepeth them, he it is that loveth me.' Peter, in his first epistle, says that it is

in our obedience that there is to be found the ultimate
fulfilment of God's redemptive purpose for our lives in and
through Jesus Christ. He says we are 'elect according to the
foreknowledge of God the Father, through sanctification of
the Spirit, unto *obedience* and sprinkling of the blood of Jesus
Christ' (1 Peter 1. 2). Here Peter is speaking about an obedience which combines both an acceptance of the cross, and an
allegiance to the Christ. Our Lord said, 'Not every one that
saith unto me, Lord, Lord, shall enter the kingdom of
heaven; but he that doeth the will of my Father which is in
heaven' (Matt. 7. 21). A life controlled by the will of God, so
that you and I can affirm, 'Thine is the kingdom . . .'

This means, first, that there will have to be *enlightenment*.
I cannot do the will of God unless I know what that will is.
So we find Paul praying for the Christians at Colosse, 'That
ye might be filled with the knowledge of His will in all
wisdom and spiritual understanding' (Col. 1. 9). And our
Lord sets out the pre-condition of such knowledge in John
7. 17, 'If any man is willing to do His will, he shall know . . .'
We must *want*, if we would know! That will mean a willingness to spend time listening, and learning what that will is; it
will mean a desire to find out what the will of God is – for my
character, for my conduct, for my career. Enlightenment:
How much time do we as Christians spend with our Bibles
every day? God has no time for those who remain lazily
ignorant of His will. Could we be described as spiritual ig-
noramuses; that we are not living in the will of God because
we don't know what that will is?

Enlightenment first; and then *involvement*. The will of
God is something to be done; it is not something simply to be
learned! It is to be lived! God's will is basically a saving will,
a redemptive will, demanding action. In the Lord's prayer
the petition has already been uttered, 'Thy will be *done*', not
suffered, not endured, but done – and done by me! Do you
remember the words of our Lord Himself? This was the
pattern of His life: 'I came not to do mine own will, but the

will of him that sent me.' And it was that will that led Him to the garden of Gethsemane, where the full implications of that obedience were presented to Him, and where victory through agony was finally His, with the words, 'Not my will, but thine be *done*'. Involvement.

Living a life controlled by the will of God means enlightenment; it means involvement; but supremely it means *enthronement*. There have been 'other lords' having dominion over us, but now it is the one Lord. And if enthroning Him is a reality, it means de-throning others. While the will of God is supremely positive, it has its negative side as well. What were the 'other Lords' that controlled our lives? In Paul's letter to the Ephesians we see, in chapter 2, what had controlled the life pattern of the Ephesian readers before they had become Christians. Paul says, 'You walked according to the course of this world'; in other words, 'What everybody else did, you did. What society, a pagan society, decreed, you obeyed.' Or if it wasn't what everybody did, Paul says of them that they walked 'fulfilling the desires of the flesh and of the mind'. In other words, he implies 'you did what you wanted'. What everybody does, what I want – society, self – these must be dethroned in order that He may be enthroned.

When Saul of Tarsus met the risen Lord, and was challenged by the vision of Christ in His glory, this was the principle he stumbled on right at the beginning of his Christian experience. Do you remember how a light 'shined round about him', and he fell to the ground, and heard a voice saying, 'Saul, Saul, why persecutest thou me?' His response was, 'Who art thou, Lord?' Now, that reads as a question all the way through, but I don't know whether it was a question all the way through! I think it was a question to begin with, and then I think the last word was one of recognition. 'Who art thou? – *Lord*! It's you!' And back came the confirming word, 'Yes, I am Jesus.' Then came the question, 'Lord, what wilt *thou* have me to do?' Here was the new will that was to direct the life of this man. Control by the will of God means enlightenment, involvement, and enthronement. 'Thine is the kingdom'.

Wasn't it Charles Finney who said that revival consists in a new obedience? When I travel the world – and that has been my privilege for many years – I honestly feel that many times I don't need to say anything at all: all that Christians need to do is to go and obey the truth we already have! 'Thine is the kingdom.' Can we look up into the face of our risen Lord, and say that – and mean it: 'Thine is the kingdom'? Enlightenment, involvement, enthronement. That's simple, isn't it? Nothing very complicated doctrinally, about that.

What's the second principle? A Christian life, if it is to be lived truly, is a life not simply controlled by the will of God, but –

CONFIDENT IN THE POWER OF GOD. 'Thine is the power.' 'Thine is the kingdom' – there is the *authority* under which I live. And I think we want to hang on to that word 'authority'. It's not liked today. But it was one way in which Jesus was described; you remember the centurion who said, 'I *also* am a man under authority.' He recognised that Jesus submitted to the authority of the Father's will. And then we find it in the Great Commission: 'All power is given unto me' – but here 'power' is not the Greek word. The Greek word is, 'All authority is given to me.' There is the authority under which we live; and 'Thine is the power' – there is the *adequacy* by which we live. I am to live confidently, in the power of God. I not only must say, 'Thine is the kingdom,' but I can say, 'Thine is the power.' What confidence marked the Early Church! What cringing hesitance marks the Church today. I want to make just three observations to expand our thinking here.

The Christian is thinking in terms of *a power that has been received*. The promise of our Lord to the Church at His ascension was crystal clear: 'Ye shall receive power after that the Holy Ghost is come upon you.' Power to stand where otherwise I would give way. Power to be what otherwise I would never be. Power to speak when otherwise I would remain silent. Power to love and care where otherwise I would remain indifferent. Power to understand, power to undertake, power to go where I would never otherwise go. Power! Every believer has received the Spirit of God. Don't get confused by the AV translation of the question put by Paul to that little group of disciples that he found at Ephesus: 'Have ye received the Holy Spirit since ye believed?' That's not how the Greek really runs, and is not what Paul actually said! What he did say was, 'Did you receive the Holy Spirit when you believed?' And they replied, 'We've never heard of the Holy Spirit.' These men were not Christians. They were simply believers in what they had already heard, which only was concerning the message of John the Baptist. I question whether they knew of the cross. They certainly didn't know of Pentecost. We don't receive the Holy Spirit *after* we're converted: we are born of the Spirit; we are sealed by the Spirit the moment we believe. That power has been received! And I want to say to every believer reading these words, you've got all the power that God can give you. And that word in the Greek is *dunamis*, from which we get our word 'dynamite'. I wonder how many Christians we know are the least little bit like dynamite!

The power has been received. But this power that has been received is *a power that must be released*. The Holy Spirit does not operate automatically. Sister Eva, of Friedenshort, speaks of the Holy Ghost as being in too many lives, 'a prisoner without power'. We have Him; we received Him; but we do not release Him. He's not allowed to do what He's been given to do. He is not allowed to be what He has been given to be. And so although we have the power, that power is not free to work in and through us.

We need to distinguish, of course, between the diversities of gifts bestowed by the Spirit, and what I like to call the ministries of grace exercised by the Spirit. There's a tremendous amount of confusion among Christians today because they don't differentiate between the two. There is a diversity of gifts that the Holy Spirit bestows of His own sovereign will. But many Christians today are insisting on uniformity. Everybody's got to have one particular gift of the Spirit, if they are really to feel that they've arrived! That is not Biblical. The Holy Spirit gives me a gift; He gives you a gift. I've no right to tell you what gift you should have, and you've no right to tell me what gift I should have. The Holy Spirit will give me mine! He will give you yours.

But the Holy Spirit has also been given to exercise certain ministries; these are things that He wants to carry out in every life. And you and I grieve the Holy Spirit when we fail to allow Him to do in us that for which He has been given. The power of the Spirit becomes experiential and evidential in our lives, not emotionally, but functionally, when He is doing what He has been given to do, and thereby is able to exercise His gracious power and influence in your life and through it.

A power that has been received; a power that must be released. But we go a step further, *a power that can be relied on.* And this is where we fall short. How immediately Peter acted upon the promise of the power of the Holy Spirit! We find him on his feet in the city where forces that had destroyed his Lord were most strongly entrenched, and counting on the faithfulness of his Lord and His Word, he spoke. How desperately the Church needs to move into the attack; how desperately we need to halt our retreat, and turn it into advance; how desperately we need to be on our feet; how desperately we need to let our faith become vocal. Why are we always on the defensive, always the ones who are willing to give way, and give in? If what we believe is right and true, and what we offer will transform and enrich the lives of men, why are we sitting in our churches waiting for them to come to us? Why do we not go to them?

The communist cause is growing by leaps and bounds, not by the meetings they hold in special buildings. They have a few no doubt; but their cause is growing by leaps and bounds, not because of the meetings they have, but because of the talking they do on the shop floor, in the factory, in the office, in the staff room at the school, in the university. They talk, talk, talk! And the Christian Church is dumb! When did we last speak to anybody about Jesus Christ? When? Here is the power that can be relied upon. And the lovely thing is this, that that power can operate through the most feeble and faltering words. A preacher can get up and preach a wonderful sermon: he's got three headings, and they all begin with the same letter – and yet that sermon can achieve absolutely nothing! And a little lass who is nothing to look at, just a scrap of a girl, can talk to a man and advise him to go to hear Billy Graham at Earls Court; and that man goes, and is converted to Christ. That little girl who invited that man didn't know that he was second-in-command of the Mafia in Europe; but he was. You don't need to be a preacher to be effective. You can make an absolute hash of an argument or a discussion on the shop floor, but the Holy Spirit doesn't mind. He will take your hashed-up defeat and turn it into victory. The Christian has power to be relied on!

So the Christian life lived normally, healthfully, growingly, developingly, is a life that is controlled by the will of God, confident in the power of God, and supremely a life that is –

CONCERNED FOR THE GLORY OF GOD. 'Thine is the kingdom, and the power, *and the glory.*' We find this concern

expressed again and again in the New Testament. In Rom.
1. 21 Paul names the root sin of the unbeliever as failure to
glorify God, to give Him His honour, the place which is His
by right, the obedience due to Him, and the praise! In 1 Cor.
6. 20 the Christians were told that their obligation was to
'glorify God in their bodies'; and again in 1 Cor. 10. 31, to
'do all to the glory of God'. In the life of our Lord this was
His own great, consuming passion: 'Father, glorify Thy
name.' In our lives there is to be a concern for the glory of
God!

Think *how shameful is the reproach done by men*, both by
unbelievers and believers, when God is defied, the Spirit is
resisted, and His Son rejected, His laws broken, His day disregarded, His house empty. Do you think an empty church
brings glory to God? I don't. When the passer-by sees folk
pouring out of church, that's more likely to bring glory to
God. Where are the folk that should be in their places every
Sunday evening? I tell you where they are. You will find
them – believers – sitting in front of a television screen,
watching a film: Christians who would never have dreamed
of going to a picture house to see it. They see it at home, on
the Lord's day when they should be in the Lord's house. Is
that glorifying God? I tell you it is not. How shameful is the
reproach done by men, when His Word is unread, His name
discredited, His Gospel misrepresented. Shameful, the reproach done!

How hurtful is the distress caused. I wonder if it was this
that really caused the Saviour to weep when He came to
Jerusalem. We are told He beheld the city and wept over it. I
don't think it was simply that judgment that He knew was
coming upon them. I think it was the dishonour, the hurt to
the heart of the God who loved them. How many of us have
varying memories; and one memory that comes back leaping
to me over the years, was the time when I found myself in
circumstances that were deliberately designed to humiliate
me. And I remember looking up at those watching around,

and I saw one face turned away, as if it could not bear the sight. How distressed you would be to see your child humiliated. Would you, if you are a parent, like to see your child treated like that? What about the way your Lord is treated today?

How powerful is the motive formed. Someone has said that a concern for the glory of God is the most powerful motivation in the work of the Christian Church. Is this our great concern, the glory of God? Is this what determines the kind of life we live, the kind of church we have, the kind of world we live in? Is this what causes you constant distress – to think that Jesus died, and these people all around are trampling the blood of Christ under their feet. Does this bother us?

For many years I have shared in what is called the Christian Holiday Crusade held at Filey in September. Each day ends with a meeting in the Gaiety Theatre, concluding with the singing of the Lord's Prayer to the music of Malotte. I find myself deeply moved as some three thousand voices join in the final tremendous crescendo, 'Thine is the kingdom, and the power, and the glory, for ever, Amen!' Sometimes I find I can scarcely sing the words, But the conviction burns deeply in my soul – that is the secret – what more do we need than that!

Surely He is worthy of glory and adoration and obedience and sacrifice! Somehow I feel if we could take these familiar words and weave them into the pattern of our living, we should find our feet on the path to a life of effectiveness and loveliness that will commend the Saviour; that will draw us together in fellowship, and draw others in, in faith. 'Thine is the kingdom': controlled by the will, of God. 'Thine is the power': confident in the power of God. 'Thine is the glory': concerned for the glory of God.

You've said those words ten thousand times. Would you be willing to say them, and mean them, and live them, and go out and find that this is the way that will bring you into fullness of life, and bring others into the same life through Christ?

Thine is the kingdom – controlled by the will of God.
Thine is the power – confident in the power of God.
Thine is the glory – concerned for the glory of God.

14

The unpardonable sin

'He that shall blaspheme against the
Holy Ghost hath never forgiveness'
(Mark 3. 29).

I OFTEN FEEL that examining the Gospel of Jesus Christ is
very like examining a jewel in one's hand, and as you turn it
this way and that, so the light catches on the various facets
of it. But sometimes if you are wanting to appreciate the
brilliance of a gem, or maybe if it is a young fellow going
in to buy an engagement ring for the girl of his choice, or
maybe the two of them doing it together – he hoping she will
keep within the price he can afford – the jeweller will take
out a dark backcloth and he will roll it out over the counter,
so that you might appreciate the gem; then he places the
gem and the ring on that dark backcloth. I am now going to
do just that and spread the dark backcloth, and lay the
Gospel on it. I want to look with you at one of the most
frightening things that Jesus Christ ever said, when He
spoke of what some have since called 'the unpardonable sin'.

One commentator says that this passage contains a dreadful warning. Let us remember that these words are Christ's
words; it is His hand that unrolls that dark, dark backcloth
to the offer of God's grace and love in Christ. The whole
matter arose out of an encounter between Christ and those

described in Mark 3. 22 as 'the scribes which came down from Jerusalem and said, 'He hath Beelzebub, and by the prince of the devils casteth he out devils'. And the conclusion that Jesus reached in the closing three verses, 'Verily I say unto you, all sins shall be forgiven unto the sons of men, and blasphemies wherewith soever they shall blaspheme: but he that shall blaspheme against the Holy Ghost hath never forgiveness, but is in danger of eternal damnation: because they said, He hath an unclean spirit.' There is the dark backcloth – as I have already suggested, it is one of the most frightening things that Jesus Christ ever said. Now there are three lines of thought that I want to note; and we will realise that although what our Lord was talking about here happened a long time ago, it can happen still! It happened in Palestine; it can happen here. First of all I want to note what I have called –

THEIR CONFRONTATION WITH JESUS CHRIST. We see these men face to face with Jesus Christ, and it was out of that encounter that the words of dreadful warning came. Let us remember this. It is speaking of a confrontation with Jesus Christ: and there are two observations that I feel I must make. The first is that *the confrontation was inevitable.* Jesus Christ just could not be ignored. Both the works that He did and the words that He said had to be taken note of. In v. 8 we are told that 'a great multitude, when they had heard what great things he did, came unto him'. The works that He did spoke of a power that He had that was more than human; and the words that He spoke claimed and indeed conveyed a sense of authority which was utterly convincing; an authority too, which could not be explained in human terms. The very evil spirits cast out by Him had named Him 'Son of God'. All this was happening in the realm of the religious life and thought in which these scribes themselves claimed to have special insight, special enlightenment, special authority. If Jesus Christ was entering the sphere of men's belief in God, then they had to take cognisance of the facts that were reported to them; facts that had set the whole nation into a fever of speculation. This confrontation was inevitable, and it still is. If men believe in God at all, if they have any interest at all in religion then Jesus Christ must be faced and encountered, and He must be explained. His words, or what He said; His works, or what He did: all these must be examined. No man ever spoke like this man. No man was ever born like this man. No man ever lived like this man. No man ever died like this man. The confrontation was inevitable. And I trust and pray that somehow God the Holy Spirit will make this day for someone a day of confrontation between you and Jesus Christ.

The second thing I would observe is that *the confrontation was uncomfortable*. Jesus Christ disturbed so many people. He disregarded so many popularly accepted ideas. He discarded so much that people had thought important, and all that with an assumption of an authority that brooked no discussion. He had not come to discuss but to declare God's truth; to display God's grace, and to demand man's total submission to both. But for so many of the scribes and Pharisees their faith in God had become identified with a mere outward observance of certain rules, with a conformity to a certain pattern of religious observance, to the use of the correct religious vocabulary. But all this had been cut down and thrown aside, and they were brought face to face with the inwardness of man's relationship to God, with what God required of man inwardly, with what man must render to God inwardly. They had to face the inwardness of it all and the thoroughness of it all. There was no place for compromise, for reservations: it was all or nothing! And the cosy, elaborate, even impressive religious structure that they had created, in which they had settled down so comfortably, was brought crashing down about their heads. Uncomfortable! Their confrontation with Jesus Christ – and it is so still. If you and I were to take the words of Jesus Christ absolutely seriously these would be the most disturbing words we could ever hear. We just couldn't go on living the way we are living.

As you know, in certain areas of the Roman Church there is a ferment of change, taking two forms: the one takes an extremely liberal view of Scripture and sweeps aside all the central doctrines of the Christian faith; the other takes a submissive and conservative view of Scripture which is bringing about a new reformation as happened in the Roman Church centuries ago and which in certain areas it is happening again today. Some time ago a leading Continental Roman Catholic priest was being interviewed by a Church of Scotland minister on television, and the Church of Scotland minister asked him, 'When can we expect in Scotland the same kind of ferment of change that you are experiencing in your country in Europe?' To which the Roman Catholic theologian replied, 'It will happen when you begin to take Jesus Christ seriously!' Their confrontation with Jesus Christ was uncomfortable, and it is with the same disturbing Christ that you and I have to do – not with me as a preacher: not with the Church as an institution: it is with Jesus Christ as the Son of God and Saviour of man.

The second thing I note is what I have called –

THEIR CONSIDERATION OF JESUS CHRIST. Thank goodness they did at least consider Him! They made the effort to come down from Jerusalem. They had heard the reports of what He had done, of what He had said, and they watched Him. Nothing is worse than total indifference: even hostility is better than apathy. These men at least gave Christ and themselves a chance to sort things out.

But even as they did so two things emerged: the first was that they were faced with *the choice that they knew they must make about Him*. The choice was a simple one. He was either of God, or He was of the devil. The Bible recognises only two realms of spiritual power – the kingdom of darkness, and the kingdom of light; and only two sources could explain the supernatural events. No man could have done what He had done – no *man* could. The choice was clear: was He God or devil? But to admit that He was the Son of God would compel them to accept His teaching; and for them to submit to His reign and to His authority would be far too costly – costly in terms of their pride, costly in terms of their pleasure, costly in terms of their pocket, costly in terms of their comfort, costly in terms of their relationships with other people in society. To admit that He was the Son of God would spell disaster to everything for which they had toiled and which they had chosen to believe. It was asking too much. But a choice had to be made. And I want to submit to you that a choice must still be made. Is Jesus Christ the Son of God? Or is He of the pit? The choice they had to make is the same choice that we have to make!

Then I note *the charge they felt they must bring against Him.* The would not admit His deity, and they had no choice but to identify Him with Satan. 'He is possessed by Beelzebub,' they said, 'and by the prince of demons he is casting out demons.' And labelling Him thus they could then wash their hands of Him and go on their own sweet way unchanged and unchanging. If He was of the devil then He had no relevance to them, for they claimed to be of God. The absurdity of their position was immediately exposed by Christ. 'How can Satan cast out Satan?' And in Matthew's account He speaks also of fruit being good on a tree, then surely the tree must be good. He appeals to logic and to reason: but sin is never either logical or reasonable. These men were concerned only to preserve the status quo in their own lives. They did not want to change anything. They wanted to avoid the disturbance that they sensed that an acceptance of the claims of Jesus Christ would entail. They wanted to remain as they were. Well, the only way they could do that was to denigrate Him! The choice was made: the charge was brought. That was their verdict! What is yours? Is He from the pit? Or is He the Son of God? Their confrontation with Him – inevitable, uncomfortable! Their consideration of Him – the choice they knew they must make: the charge that they felt they must bring.

Finally we see –

THEIR CONDEMNATION BY JESUS CHRIST. Let me read how this verse is translated in the Amplified New Testament, which tries to penetrate behind the actual Greek to the sense of it. 'Truly and solemnly I say to you. All sin will be forgiven the sons of men, and whatever abusive and blasphemous things they utter; but whoever speaks abusively against or maliciously represents the Holy Spirit can never get forgiveness, but is guilty of, and is in the grasp of *an everlasting trespass*,' or as the Revised Standard Version translates it, 'is guilty of *an eternal sin*'. Now, note that these words were spoken to unbelievers. I have from time to time come across Christians who think they have committed what they call 'the unpardonable sin'. I want to say with the utmost conviction that it is impossible for a Christian to commit the unpardonable sin: a Christian cannot do it – but a church member can! Because, you see, you can be a member of a church and an unbeliever! What is it all about, this sin that leads to 'the land of no forgiveness'? It is what is called the eternal or the everlasting sin. *And because the sin, if persisted in, is eternal and everlasting, so the place of forgiveness is never found*. Note further that Jesus didn't say that these scribes, these unbelievers had actually committed it, but their attitude made Him warn them of its existence. His words are *a warning against something that is possible*. What is it? It is a persistent and maintained refusal to accept the claims of Jesus Christ: that is the sin that can last so long in a man's life – indeed, right to the very end of that life – that it may finally merit the description of 'the eternal sin'! These scribes persisted in their refusal to acknowledge that

Christ was who He was; that the work He did was a divine work. They said that to them it was the work of the devil. I have said, and I repeat it, that no Christian can commit this sin, this blasphemy; no Christian can take up this attitude, but an unbeliever can. It is something that is possible, a persistence in an attitude, which means in effect that you turn your back upon Jesus Christ and walk and walk away from Him and away from His truth, away from His grace and away from His cross. If you turn your back on Jesus Christ knowing Him to be who He is, and if you are still walking that way when death comes you will continue walking that way into the land of 'no forgiveness'.

No forgiveness! Here is something that is possible. Here too is a warning against *something that is terrible*: 'hath never forgiveness'. Sometimes people talk as if all men are journeying the same road and that when we die all men reach the same destination. May I say this is not the teaching of Jesus Christ. There *is* a land of no forgiveness, there *is* a place of outer darkness: but if men end there it is their own desire, and not God's. At every turn God's love and God's Spirit will try to turn us from that path; but if we persist, if we go on refusing through to the bitter end, the choice and the place is our own – not God's. I don't believe that God sends anybody to hell. But if a man insists on going there, not even God can stop him! The way to go there is to continue to reject, to resist and refuse God's offer in Jesus Christ, to turn your back upon Him and go on living that way, and in the end dying that way, with your back turned upon Jesus Christ! But if you do get there, on the way you will pass churches by the score. You will pass the Word of God, the memory of a thousand voices will have to be silenced, the example of a hundred Christian friends will have to go unheeded, the experiences of life, of joy, of sorrow, intended by God and used by the Holy Spirit to bring us to Himself, will have to be forgotten. No, if we have set our faces away from Christ, away from the cross, away from His word, away from

His will, if we are determined that we are going to live and
die apart from Him, *that* is the road to 'the land of no forgiveness'. Everything that the Holy Spirit has revealed to us
of Christ has been brushed aside. We have trampled under
our feet the very cross of Christ. This is the road we have
decided to take, and in the taking of it, if we persist to the
very end we will wake up in eternity and find that we have
committed what the Bible calls 'the sin that hath never forgiveness'. Do you wonder that I call it one of the most frightening things that Jesus Christ ever said.

What a dark, black backcloth, to the glory of the Gospel;
and yet even when our Lord is spreading out this dark backcloth He doesn't leave it without the sparkling flashing gem
of His grace, right in the centre. Listen! 'Verily (truly) I say
unto you, All sins shall be forgiven unto the sons of men.'
There it is, the forgiveness of God; that gift of God's love
that meant a giving of His Son to the death of the cross, and
then a giving of His Son to us now by the Holy Spirit – the
gift of His Son. What more could God do than He has done?
I don't know what else He could do, do you? He has made
possible a new relationship, with the sin on my conscience
and on my heart lifted right off me and blotted out, because
of the death of Jesus Christ! What a fantastic gift that is! A
new relationship with God. When the Jubilee Singers, an
American Negro group, came over to Britain many years
ago, they used to sing –

> My sins are blotted out I know,
> My sins are blotted out I know:
> They are buried in the depths of the deepest sea;
> My sins are blotted out, I know.

This is what the forgiveness of sins means – a new relationship with God, because the whole sin question had been resolved and swept away! When the veil of the temple was
torn from the top to the bottom, at the moment when Christ

died, it meant the way through was now open so that sinful men could live in the presence of God whoever they were and wherever they are. But beyond the new relationship there would be the new resources. Man needs so much more than forgiveness; we need strength, we need wisdom, we need courage, we need love: and all this is given to me and offered to me in the person of the risen Christ. Could God do more than that? I don't know what else He could do! And added to that, what shall I say of the constant striving of the Holy Spirit to bring me to see my need and to seek Christ as the answer to it? God has been at work ever since you were born to bring you to Christ. What more could He do? Did He give you a godly father and a godly mother who prayed for you; Sunday-school teachers, Christian friends, members of your own family, a godly minister preaching the Word? What else could God do? Tell me? Now if you throw it all back in God's face, whose fault is it, God's? No! It is your own fault! You have nobody else to blame except yourself! God doesn't want you to go this road, but He didn't make you a puppet, He made you a person and you have got the right to choose.

Just before the Mau Mau trouble broke out in Nairobi I was taking a teaching mission there in the cathedral. I had booklets available after each service, to help and guide those who wanted help: and people could ask for these each night during the fortnight's mission. But when it came to the final service I had another book, a bigger book that I felt some of those who had been seeking or who had found Christ as Saviour might find helpful. I felt too that if they were willing to come forward they could make the receiving of that book an act of open witness that they were now Christ's. The first person coming up that aisle was a white-haired man with the tears just streaming down his face. I couldn't help thinking what a long time it had taken the good Lord to bring that man to Himself! How long has He been trying to persuade you, to convince you that you can trust Jesus

Christ without any fear? And here you are, still swithering. Should I say, 'yes'? Should I say, 'no'?

So I want you to consider the gem you have been looking at. Some of you have been looking at it long enough. You have seen the facets of God's light and God's love and God's truth shine in the Gospel of Jesus Christ, and deep down in your heart you have said, 'My, that's it: that's tremendous: that's real: that's true: that's wonderful. I would like to know that in my own life.' You have said it, but you haven't done it. And how yet again the good Lord is speaking to you. Would it not be tremendous if this long, long business of running away from God suddenly came to an end? Have you seen a small child running away from its dad? Stupid wee thing! And there's the father running after it – or the mother, and finally the wee one is captured and the arms of love are round, and that little one is picked up and taken into safety and security! That is what the arms of the love of God would love to do to you today! Will you commit your life to Christ? Will you make that choice that you know is the right one? You have considered Christ. Why not make that right decision and say 'yes, it is the only thing we can reasonably and rationally do!' Will you say, 'He died for me. I know He died for me. He rose again, He is alive, and wants to come into my life. I know He wants to come. I will let Him.' Ask Him to come in, and He will come. Say, 'Come in, Lord,' and so enter into that new relationship with God, and begin to enjoy the new resources that Christ will bring into your life. Will you do it? There's the sparkling gem, the flashing jewel. The gift of God's love to you; but you need to take it. Will you take it now? Not it – but *Him.*

15

His claim to set men free

'If the Son shall make you free, you shall
be free indeed' (John 8. 36).

I WANT TO think out with you this fantastic claim that
Jesus Christ makes to make men free, or as J. B. Phillips
translates it, 'really free', and I want to ask just exactly what
Christ's freedom really means.

Freedom is one of the words that is constantly on the lips
and in the minds of people today. We talk about it, we even
sing about it. Cliff Richard has a song about freedom, titled
'Sing a Song of Freedom'. People are not only talking about
freedom, they are claiming it, they are seeking it. But when
we look more closely into so much of the talk, we find that
there is a great deal that is superficial and indeed utterly
false. The Bible has a devastating sentence describing so ac-
curately the situation in the lives of so many people. Peter
writes of those who promise freedom to others but they
themselves are slaves (2 Peter 2. 19). Freedom is not quite so
easily found as we might like to think. We know of course
what some people want freedom from. They want freedom
from authority, whether that authority is in government, in
schools or in homes. We know that there are financial

interests that want freedom from censorship. People want freedom from restraint. But what do they want freedom for? Do they want to be free to exploit the weaknesses of others, freedom to indulge their own selfish desires? Do they want to be free to gratify their own lusts and passions? Do they want freedom for themselves irrespective of the fact that their freedom might injure others? And in the final analysis is the freedom they talk about and indeed may boast about, really freedom? Let us then try to think out what kind of freedom Jesus Christ will give to those who commit their lives to Him.

In John's Gospel 8. 31–36 there is a short passage which throws light upon the freedom that makes men 'really free', and from these words of Jesus Christ, I want to suggest that the freedom that Christ gives is, first of all –

FREEDOM FROM THE BLUNDERS THAT CAN BLIGHT A MAN'S LIFE. In v. 31 Christ says, 'If ye continue in my word, then are ye my disciples indeed; and ye shall know the truth, and the truth small make you free.' Think for a moment of *the decisions our lives will hold*: decisions that we cannot avoid, and decisions which when we make them, are so often wrong. Some of the decisions may not be so very important, but some are quite crucial. We have to make decisions about matters of right or wrong, decisions about where happiness is to be found, decisions about marriage, decisions about our future. We have to decide what are we going to do with our lives. We have to make up our minds what are we going to do with our time, with our money, and possibly the biggest decision of all, what are we going to do about God. There are so many decisions we just cannot avoid: we have to make them, but alas, so often we find that the decisions we have made have been wrong!

One of the great hymn-writers has described time as 'like an ever rolling stream', and indeed it is, because we cannot halt time; and as time carries us along so we must choose.

We must decide – and even when we fail to choose or decide, we have in effect chosen and decided! And how deceptive so often life can prove. In making the decisions we did, we were so sure that we were right, that we would find happiness along this road: but we did not, and time has proved that we were wrong although we were quite sure we were right! So we have to take into account the decisions that our lives will hold. There is no use rebelling against this. This is in the very nature of man. He has been created a moral being with the power and the right to choose, but the tragedy is that so often when we are wrong, the blunder does indeed blight a man's life. I have never forgotten calling on a man who had started coming to one of my churches. When I called at his home I found him alone, his wife and daughter were out. We talked for a while, and then he said something to me that I have never forgotten. He said, 'You know, Mr. Duncan, I haven't darkened the door of a church for thirty years; and for thirty years,' he added, 'I have been wrong!' I have never forgotten the sense of tragedy and pathos behind those last words 'for thirty years I have been wrong!' What a tragic blunder to have wasted thirty years out of a life!

But if you and I have to face the fact of the decisions our lives will hold, when we come face to face with Jesus Christ we find that He is making a claim to set us free, free from the blunders that can blight a man's life, because of *the direction our lives can have*. For into my ignorance and my uncertainty comes Jesus Christ with His fantastic claim, 'If ye continue in my word, then are ye my disciples indeed; and ye shall know the truth, and the truth shall make you free.' He had already made that tremendous claim, 'I am the light of the world: he that followeth me shall not walk in darkness, but shall have the light of life' (John 8. 12). And again, Christ says, 'I am the way, the truth, and the life' (John 14. 6). In Christ there is the truth we need, and the light we need – the truth about God and about man; the truth about life and about death, about what is right and what is wrong.

Just as a light will show me the path I should follow and the perils and dangers I should avoid, so what Christ has to tell me will direct me, if I choose to follow, into the quality of life which will hold that fullness and freedom which is what God has planned for every one of us. Is that freedom not something worth having? When I remember that I have only one life to live, and that if I spoil that one life I haven't another, can I afford to take the risk of messing it up as so many have done? Indeed, so many of those who have turned their backs on the light of the truth that Jesus Christ sheds, have ended by getting desperately hurt and sometimes utterly lost, so much so that they reach the final blundering decision that life is no longer worth living and end their lives – at least, their lives on earth!

A well-known personality in the entertainment world, Judy Garland, made this final blundering decision. In her early days she was famous for a song she used to sing which included the words, 'Somewhere over the rainbow skies are blue'. But it would appear that Judy Garland never reached that somewhere, and never found those blue skies, although she had fame and wealth and position and what the world would call success. Freedom from the blunders that can blight a man's life. 'If the Son shall make you free, you shall be free indeed!' But there is another freedom that Christ would claim to give, I have called it –

FREEDOM FROM THE BURDEN THAT CAN BREAK A MAN'S HEART. Jesus Christ described men as 'heavy laden', carrying loads that were too heavy for them to bear. John Bunyan, in that matchless allegory of human life called *Pilgrim's Progress*, described the man who became the pilgrim as 'having a great burden upon his back'. The writer of one of our lovely Christmas carols has the same insight, and writes of those 'beneath life's crushing load', whose 'forms are bending low, who toil along the climbing way with painful steps and slow'. 'Heavy laden', 'a great burden', 'life's crushing load'. Three witnesses out of the thousands we could call to suggest that there are burdens that can and do break a man's heart: and yet Christ comes in with this tremendous claim, 'if I the Son of God shall make you free, you shall be free indeed.'

I want us to note that there is *a burden that man cannot bear*. What is the thing that so often breaks the heart of a man? There is one thing above all others that constitutes a load too heavy for any individual to attempt to carry. It is the burden of the guilt of sin; and this I affirm in spite of the fact that we live in an age that almost would abolish guilt as simply a stupid bit of human imagination. With all the glib talk however about being free to do as we like, people are discovering that they are not free to do what they like without involving themselves in consequences which are quite beyond their control, and one of these consequences is the way in which sin fastens upon us a sense of guilt that we cannot shake off.

The great American preacher, Dr. Fosdick, has a devastating paragraph in one of his books. He writes, 'Simple pleasure lures us only in anticipation, dancing before us like Salome before her uncle Herod quite irresistible in fascination. Happiness seems altogether to depend upon an evil deed; but on the day that deed long held in alluring expectation is actually done, how swift and terrible the alteration in its aspect! It passes from anticipation, through committal, into memory, and it will never be beautiful again! We lock it in remembrance as in the bloody room of Blue Beard's palace where the dead things hang. At the thought of it we shrink, and yet to it our reminiscence is continually drawn. Something happens in us as automatic as the dropping of a loosened apple from a tree; all the laws of the moral universe conspire to further it, and we have no power to prevent it. Sin becomes guilt.'

Michael Green in one of his books recalls an incident during a mission in one of our British universities, when a girl who was notorious in the university for her fast way of life, came up to speak to him. She looked the way she lived, as hard as nails! She told Michael Green she wanted to become a Christian and take Christ into her life. He could hardly believe that she meant what she was saying, but he counselled her and showed her how simply Christ could come into her life if she wanted Him and would welcome Him. The next day she came to him again. Michael Green says there already seemed to be a difference in her very appearance, but the significant thing that he recalled was what she said to him. She said how that all the time she had been living the way of life she had been living – and there was little she didn't know about drink or drugs or men – 'All that time,' she said, 'I felt as guilty as hell.'

Dr. Fosdick states, 'When on the lonely ocean the floating bell-buoy tolls, no human hands will cause it to ring the wastes of an unpeopled ocean surrounding it in every way, but the sea by its own restlessness is ringing its own bell. So tolls remorse in a man's heart, and no man can stop it.' I remember hearing of a clergyman visiting one of our large mental hospitals, and how the doctor taking him round said to him, 'Half of my patients could be out of here if they could only find the secret of forgiveness.' David, the man after God's own heart, acknowledged, 'My sin is ever before me.' Here indeed is a burden that man cannot bear! But when we face the person of Jesus Christ, we discover that He can give us freedom from that burden, because we learn from Him that this is *a burden a man need not bear*. And the reason we need not bear it is because He has borne it for us. His words still ring down over the centuries, 'Come unto me, all ye that labour and are heavy laden, and I will give you rest.'

Away back centuries before Christ came, a prophet foretold the day in which Christ would come, a day in which Christ would die; and this is what that prophet said that death would signify: 'All we like sheep have gone astray;

we have turned every one to his own way; and the Lord hath laid on him the iniquity of us all. He was wounded for our transgressions, he was bruised for our iniquities; the chastisement of our peace was upon him; and with his stripes we are healed.' And if our iniquities were laid upon Him, it means surely that they have been lifted away from us. When that Christ, foretold centuries before He came, finally did come, the last prophet, John the Baptist, identified Him on the banks of the Jordan with the words, 'Behold the Lamb of God, which beareth away the sins of the world.' If He is bearing my guilt, then I need bear it myself no longer! One of the so-called old-fashioned Gospel hymns puts it in unforgettable words –

> My sin – oh, the bliss of this glorious thought –
> My sin, not in part, but the whole,
> Is nailed to His cross, and I bear it no more,
> Praise the Lord, praise the Lord, oh, my soul.

This is the burden I need not bear because He has borne it for me! It was when John Bunyan's pilgrim came to that hill, that place 'somewhat ascending', and saw at the top of it a cross, that the burden he was bearing 'loosed from off his back' and fell into an open sepulchre. And John Bunyan adds the wonderful words, 'and I saw it no more'! There is an old chorus that some of us love to sing which expresses this in some wonderful words –

> I know a fount where sins are washed away;
> I know a place where night is turned to day;
> Burdens are lifted, blind eyes made to see:
> There's a wonder-working power in the blood of Calvary.

Free indeed from the blunders that blight a man's life; free from the burden that can break a man's heart! But there is one other freedom to which Christ refers in these verses in John 8. I call it –

FREEDOM FROM THE BONDAGE THAT CAN BIND A MAN'S SOUL. Just two verses back from our text is another of the statements of Jesus Christ, 'Whosoever committeth sin is the slave of sin (v. 34). We like to think we are free to do as we like, and on that principle we act, only to wake up to the fact that while we may think we are free to do as we like, we are not free to stop doing it! When Jesus Christ commenced His ministry, when He was reading the lesson in the synagogue, He quoted an Old Testament prophecy and identified His own mission with those words, that He had come 'to preach deliverance to the captives, to set at liberty them that are bruised'. Here is freedom from the bondage that can bind a man's soul.

I note two things that shed light upon this aspect of Christian freedom. First, *the tyranny imposed by sin*. In the psalms, David, the man after God's own heart, cries out, 'Mine iniquities prevail against me.' Someone has translated those words much more vividly: 'My sins are mightier than I.' The power of sin is simply a fact of experience. We find that so many of those that talk about freedom certainly don't demonstrate it. We find that they live lives in bondage to habits they cannot break. How do the words run – 'Sow a thought, reap an act; sow an act, reap a habit; sow a habit, reap a character; sow a character, reap a destiny.' Sow an act, reap a habit! Paul describes it so vividly in Rom. 7. 19, 'The good that I would I do not, but the evil that I would not I do.' But the power of sin in our lives can be seen not simply in our bondage to habits we cannot break, but in bondage to opinion that we dare not flout: our bondage to the opinions of others. In the book of wisdom that we call Proverbs there is another tremendous statement which reads, 'The fear of man bringeth a snare.' And how many of

those who would talk about being free are nevertheless
chained to the chariot wheels of public opinion, as the pris-
oners taken captive in war by Roman generals would be
chained to the chariot wheels of their conquerors when the
triumphant army returned to Rome. How often we find ourselves wanting to do something and yet too scared to do it
because of what people would say – and yet we call that
freedom! That's not freedom, that is bondage, slavery of the
most debasing kind.

Possibly more significant still is the fact that we find ourselves so often in bondage not only to habits we cannot
break, not only to opinion that we dare not flout, but in
bondage to consequences we cannot undo, consequences that
are completely beyond our control. This again is simply a
fact of experience. The Bible puts it very bluntly in pretty
shattering words: 'Be not deceived; God is not mocked; for
whatsoever a man soweth, that shall he also reap.' Professor
Henry Drummond, who exercised such a great influence on
the students of his day, used to say, 'We not only sow, we
have to watch it grow, we see it ripen, and then we have to
reap it.' And not only do we reap, but so often others have to
share in the reaping of a bitter harvest. Life is not composed
of a series of unrelated words and deeds, but of a vitally
interrelated number of causes and effects. Someone has put
it, 'Sin always comes disguised as liberty. Its lure is the se-
ductive freedom which it promises from the trammels of
conscience and the authority of law. But every man who has
ever yet accepted sin's offer of a free unfettered life has discovered the cheat. Free to do the evil thing, the base thing,
so men begin; but they end not free to stop. They find themselves bound as slaves to the thing they thought they were
free to do.' The tyranny imposed by sin lies in the consequences I cannot undo!

When we were young as a family our parents used to take
us for holidays up into the Scottish Highlands. Speyside was

a favourite haunt. We couldn't afford a car, but we all rode bicycles and we got to know the countryside intimately. What lovely, healthy holidays they were! Playing golf and tennis on the local course and courts! Walking, climbing, fishing, bicycling! Sometimes when we had made our way through one of the forests, the Rothiemurchus Forest maybe, we would come across a small stretch of water – a lochan, it would be called in Scotland – and there on a still summer's day in the still surface of the lochan there would be reflected all the beauty of the heather and bracken, the silver birch and dark pine trees, maybe the shoulder of some great mountain, the blue of the sky and the white clouds racing across the sky, all reflected as if in a mirror! Boy-like we would pick up a stone and throw it right into the centre of the small pool of water. It would fall with a splash and immediately the picture would be shattered! I suppose it would be possible to get the stone out again if you could find it, but nothing would ever stop the ripples spreading. And life is like that! Free, really free? Not a bit of it! There is a tyranny imposed by sin. So often we are in bondage to habits we cannot break, to opinion we dare not flout, to consequences we cannot undo!

But if there is a tyranny imposed by sin there is also *a liberty enjoyed through Christ*. For the ultimate relevance of the message of Jesus Christ takes me of course to the cross where He died for my sins, but it takes me beyond the cross to the Christ who faces me in His risen power, wanting to come into my life in all the fullness of that power, to bring into my life the resources that I need! The Christ who died on the cross *is* the Christ for me, for in Him and through His death I find pardon for my sins. But the Christ who would dwell in the heart is also the Christ for me, for in that living presence I find the power I need to conquer sin. In Rom. 5. 10, St. Paul puts it so simply: 'If, when we were enemies, we were reconciled to God by the death of his Son, much more, being reconciled, we shall be saved by his life.' We shall be saved not by the example of His life, but by the experience of His life, the acceptance of His life into our lives by His Spirit!

At the beginning of his Gospel, St. John writes these tremendous words: 'To as many as received him to them he gave the power to become the sons of God.' What did John mean by 'receiving Him'? Surely not a physical receiving of Him limited to those years of active ministry, but surely it meant receiving Him as the person He was, the person He is. And in the light of the complete revelation of Christ we know that He is the Son of God, not only who died, but who lives.

One of the great hymns of Charles Wesley has a tremendous verse. The hymn begins with the words –

> And can it be, that I should gain
> An interest in the Saviour's blood . . .

One verse runs like this –

> Long my imprisoned spirit say
> Fast bound in sin and nature's night;
> Thine eyes diffused a quickening ray,
> I woke, the dungeon flamed with light:
> My chains fell off, my heart was free,
> I rose, went forth, and followed thee.

Free from the bondage that can bind a man's soul. Free to do the will of God, and to find that that will is good and perfect and therefore acceptable. 'If the Son shall make you free, you shall be free indeed.' That was the claim that Christ made, and that is the freedom that millions have found. Free from blunders that can blight a man's life; from the burden that can break a man's heart; from the bondage that can bind a man's soul. I believe that on the tombstone that marks the grave of Martin Luther King there are three words,

'Free at last'. We know what those words signify, and to what they refer, but I want to suggest that there is a freedom which we are meant to know on earth, while we are living, and not simply a freedom that we will find when we have died. It is a freedom that we find in Christ when we receive Him to be who He is, to dwell in our lives where He longs to dwell.

In the memorable sermon that Malcolm Muggeridge preached in St. Giles' Cathedral entitled 'Another King', he ended by recalling the experience which would seem to have crystallised for him the reality of Christ to meet his own needs. He recalled his visit to the Holy Land, and how he and his legal assessor Alan Fraser visited Emmaus, in these words, 'As my friend and I walked along the road to Emmaus, like Cleopas and his friend, we recalled as they did the events of the crucifixion and its aftermath in the light of our utterly different, yet strangely similar world. Nor was it fancy that we too were joined by a third presence. And I tell you that wherever the walk, and whoever the wayfarers, there is always this third presence ready to emerge from the shadows and fall in step along the dusty, stony way.' If the Son shall make you free, you shall be free indeed. Really free!

16

Religious sins

'Woe unto you ... hypocrites!' (Luke
11. 42, 43, 44, 46, 47, 52).

I REMEMBER BEING asked some years ago to address a
gathering of very distinguished and experienced men of
God. In my sense of need I turned, as is always wise to do, to
the Word of God, and scanned this passage in St. Luke's
Gospel, 11. 37–54. It suddenly came home to me with a sense
of shock that our Lord here is describing what we might call
peculiarly the sins of religious life, and that these areas of
failure are with us still today. They are in a very real sense
aspects of Christian living that need to be pin-pointed and
then dealt with, in our own hearts. I am sure that we would
resent it if somebody came up and called us Pharisees! It is a
word that has a stigma attached to it. We talk about people
as being Pharisees, and it is almost a term of contempt. But
the thing that shook me was that when I finished reading
this passage, I found that the Lord was taking the word
'Pharisee' and sticking it right across my own life. I wonder
if there isn't more of the Pharisee in religious life than sometimes we are prepared to admit. Six times over Jesus says
'Woe unto you,' and if we can take the principles that lie
behind the language, I think we will find that the sins of the
Pharisees and religious leaders of our Lord's day are still the

sins in the religious life of our day. Look at v. 42, 'Woe unto you, Pharisees'; v. 43, 'Woe unto you'; v. 44, 'Woe unto you'; v. 46, 'Woe unto you'; v. 47, 'Woe unto you'; v. 52, 'Woe unto you'. Now let us take each verse in turn and ask ourselves what is really the sin that Lord is dealing with, admittedly under a local and historical setting. In v. 42 we see what I call –

THE SIN OF STRESSING THE UNIMPORTANT. I wonder what you would say is the sin of v. 42? 'Woe unto you, Pharisees! for ye tithe mint and rue and all manner of herbs, and pass over (or disregard) judgment and the love of God: these ought ye to have done, and not to leave the other undone.' Now I suggest that the sin that our Lord is dealing with here, is the sin of stressing the unimportant. Our Lord is not saying that details do not matter. He is very careful to say, 'These ought ye to have done.' The details do matter, but they are not to matter to the exclusion of matters of much greater importance. The Pharisee in religious life is the person who stresses detail and the comparatively unimportant. I wonder if I may give you an illustration which has a local setting. In Great Britain, as in every country that I know of, there are certain things that are supposed to be done and not done by keen Christians. One matter of a very personal nature that used to be traditionally maintained (it is not so much now), was that a Christian lady did not use overmuch in the way of cosmetics! That is to say, that she did not paint her lips unduly, if at all! She was, apparently, allowed to powder her nose, but to paint on her lips was rather a different matter! In this connection a rather amusing incident occurred in the preaching ministry of my friend the Rev. Alan Redpath when on a visit to the Republic of Ireland. When the Irish Republic broke away from the United Kingdom, as part of the stress on their independence from the British throne, they painted their pillar boxes a different colour from what they had traditionally been.

From red, the Irish painted all their pillar boxes green – leaving incidentally the royal insignia GR still engraved on them! Dr. Redpath had forgotten this, and in an address he was making some reference to ladies painting their lips, and he said, 'I'm sure that God did not mean us to have our lips painted the colour of pillar boxes!' Of course the audience burst into laughter: ladies with green lips sounded quite fantastic! But the point I am getting to, is this. I used to find that some Christians who could get very worked up about the presence of paint on the lips of professing Christians were not the least concerned about the absence of prayer from their own lips. Which is more important – paint on or prayer off?

It is so possible to be absorbed with a detail, and lose sight of matters of much greater magnitude. The detail may be in the creed of the Christian, it may be in the conduct of a Christian, it may be in the character of a Christian, and the sin lies in our being absorbed with detail. I can remember being severely rebuked unconsciously by an absolute saint of God, Brother Edward, who was one of the most Christlike men I ever met, although he was not of my particular theological school of thought. He stayed with two charming friends of mine. I was younger in those days, and as young people always do, I got these two friends labelled. The lady was converted and very keen, at the top of the class; her husband was much lower down in the class, in my evaluation! After this saint of God had stayed with these two people, when we were chatting one day he said some very kind words about his hostess which I quite anticipated, and then he said this about his host: 'You know, Mr. So-and-so's humility must be greatly pleasing to our Lord.' I never looked for that humility, and I had never seen it because I was absorbed with details of language and of creed, and I had not been able to see the magnitude of the evidence of the fruit of the Spirit in that man's character. I want to suggest to you that you interpret and apply this within your own context and your

own relationships. I want you just to check up and find out
how often you and I become obsessed with a detail, and lose
sight of something of much greater magnitude. Think of the
redemptive purpose of God, how great that is! It does not
matter which instrument is used as long as the redemptive
purpose is being forwarded. Think of the will of God in that
wide scope, think of the glory of God. Then your feelings and
mine do not matter. Think of the unity of the Spirit. I have
come across some Christians who think that disunity is a
mark of sanctity. Not a bit of it. It is an evidence of sin. Nine
times out of ten it is sin on one side or on the other. There is
a basic unity of the Spirit that we are meant to enjoy! Let us
hold on to the magnitudes of our faith, and let us not become
obsessed with details to their exclusion. That is one of the
sins of the Pharisee. Let us see that the really big issues domi-
nate our thinking and absorb our attention – stressing the
unimportant: that is the first sin! In v. 43 our Lord pin-
points another sin, I call it –

THE SIN OF SEEKING THE UNMERITED. Would you say that
this was the sin the Lord was getting at, when He said, 'Woe
unto you, Pharisees! for ye love the uppermost seats in the
synagogues, and greetings in the market.' I would suggest to
you that is just what our Lord was getting at here, the sin of
seeking the unmerited. These men wanted prominence and
position before men, and our Lord is by implication saying,
'And you have not the qualifications for it.'

There is such a thing as ambition within the realm of
Christian experience, is there not? I find that there are men
who are ambitious in the realm of advancement within their
own church. They covet positions of influence and power.
They like to be chairmen of committees; they like to be
leaders. They are not content to serve, but they must be in
command. They must be obeyed. Their ideas must be the
ideas that everybody else accepts, and they are not prepared
to accept anything less. We can have an even more subtle

ambition – the ambition for spiritual power, not simply so
that God may be glorified, but so that our name will be
magnified. There is nothing that some preachers like more
than for somebody to come after a service and say, 'I did
appreciate your message. It was a blessing to my soul'; and if
nobody comes and says that, then they are greatly distressed.
This is the kind of ambition that men can foster; but there is
the condition that man can forget, which is that there is
always a spiritual price for spiritual power. What our Lord
was getting at here, was that the 'Pharisee' mind is concerned with the position and not with the condition! All he
wants is prominence before men, praise from men, albeit
Christian men, but he is not concerned at all with whether or
not he is really qualified for it, whether he is really paying
the price of spiritual power in his own heart and life. This is
seeking the unmerited.

Are you and I ever guilty of that sin? If I know anything
of my own heart, and if I know anything of the hearts of
God's people, I would suggest that this sin is much more
common than we think, and it almost always emerges when
we are denied the prominence and the position we are covet-
ing. May I take an illustration? Forgive me if I refer to my
own experience, but it sometimes helps if we can share these
things that we have gone through. When I went to college I
did my Arts course first, and then for two years I did Christian work. God was graciously pleased to bless my ministry,
no doubt in a very small way, and although I was just a
youngster and nothing very much in the way of a preacher,
God blessed what I did. I can look back on some campaigns
that I had in my early twenties, on which God set His seal.
After I had done Christian work like that for a while, I felt
the need for theological training, and I went to the Anglican
theological college in Bristol, Tyndale Hall, now Trinity
College. Part of our training was for eight of us to go out
on tour together in evangelistic outreach in the summer
vacation. We would go into a parish for an evangelistic

campaign and then on to another parish for another campaign, and the responsibility of preaching was shared between the students. I think it would be true to say that I was probably the most experienced of a rather inexperienced bunch of men, but I always remember what happened in one parish when we came to the last night of the campaign. The last night is a very important night in an evangelistic campaign, possibly the most important, and you will never believe it, but I was not asked to give the address! Although there I was with my experience, and my modest gifts, yet somebody else was given that task! I can remember yet the feeling of resentment that for a moment tended to boil up in my heart – why? Because there was a prominence and a position that I wanted. There was more of the Pharisee in me even then than I dreamed. Is there anything of the Pharisee in you? That sin shows itself when we are denied the thing that we do not think we really want, but all the time we do – that is, prominence and position, praise and acclamation from Christian people. That is the Pharisee seeking the unmerited. In v. 44 our Lord deals with what I have called –

THE SIN OF CONCEALING THE UNWORTHY. Stressing the unimportant, seeking the unmerited. Is this what you would say about v. 44? 'Woe unto you, scribes and Pharisees, hypocrites! for ye are as graves which appear not, and the men that walk over them are not aware of them.' This is the third sin of the Pharisee named by Christ and the colour darkens! I think at the back of our Lord's mind, surely, there is the thought here, not only of concealment, but of condonement. This is a condition that the Pharisee allows to go on, and on, and on. On the surface there is nothing to suggest that within there is the vilest corruption. Now I stress the fact that this is not simply a condition concealed, but a condition condoned, because every one of us is aware that in our flesh – in ourselves apart from Christ – 'there dwelleth no good thing'. God save us from ever thinking we are anything! But that is not what our Lord is dealing with here. He is dealing with a condition which is condoned and allowed to go on. On the surface there is the green grass, but beneath that, rotting corruption! 'Is this really possible in a religious life?' Well, is it? Our Lord would suggest that it is, and I do not think any of us with experience of the Christian Church or of our own hearts, but would say 'Amen!' This is true. This is possible. The very fact that a person is a Christian, the very fact that a person may hold a position, carries with it the subtle danger of thinking that a person can get away with almost anything, provided that it is never known! That is the sin of the Pharisee, concealing the unworthy! I wonder whether the 'Pharisee' is not becoming the kind of label that some of us have more right to than maybe we thought we had.

The next sin hits even harder. In v. 46 our Lord speaks of –

THE SIN OF PREACHING THE UNFULFILLED. Is this not what our Lord has in mind when He said, 'Woe unto you also, ye lawyers! for ye lade men with burdens grievous to be borne, and ye yourselves touch not the burdens with one of your fingers.' Stressing the unimportant, seeking the unmerited, concealing the unworthy – and now what I have called 'preaching the unfulfilled'. Here is the thought, first of all, of an obligation laid upon the hearer, and then of an obedience withheld by the preacher. 'Ye lade men with burdens grievous to be borne, and ye yourselves' – you do not even lift a little finger to carry that burden. What our Lord is getting at is this – which do we find easier, to preach a sermon on prayer, or to pray? Do you see that the 'Pharisee' mentality lays a burden upon other people, a burden which he has no intention of carrying himself, and does not make any attempt to carry. I wonder how many of us who are preachers have pleaded with our people that they should be obedient to the will of God, and yet all the time we are disobeying

God in some realm of our lives. We may know perfectly well that we are disobeying the will of God over some matter, and at the same time have no intention whatsoever of obeying God over it. We are in fact asking our people to do something we are not doing ourselves. I often feel that this is possibly the root sin of the Christian in his relationships to the world outside. We condemn people because they will not obey the Gospel, and yet we with our infinitely greater knowledge of God's love and grace in Christ, are not obeying His will. We are laying burdens upon others grievous for them to bear, but we ourselves are not carrying them. Preaching the unfulfilled. Please don't misunderstand me. I do not say necessarily that those of us who are preachers or teachers are not to preach something that is beyond the realm of our experience. I would not say that we are to confine ourselves to our own experience of Christ – that would be a very poor subject for preaching. But if something is not within our experience, surely it ought to be within the realm of our aspiration. If we have not got there, we ought to be striving to get there at least, before we ask others.

In v. 47 our Lord deals with what I have called –

THE SIN OF REVERENCING THE UNWANTED. I wonder if this is what you would say our Lord had in mind. 'Woe unto you! for ye build the sepulchres of the prophets, and your fathers killed them.' Matthew adds, 'and garnish – or decorate, make ornate – the graves and sepulchres of the prophets that your fathers killed'. I think what our Lord is meaning, in effect, is, 'If the prophets were alive today, you would do the same.' I feel that the sin of the Pharisees and in the religious life today, is the sin of reverencing the unwanted. I think now of a great church. It had a great minister, and if I mentioned his name anybody with a Scottish background would know the church. He was a great preacher, and he was the man whose ministry put this church right on the map. He had a great insight into human sin and the human heart. I do not say this situation exists in this church, but it is the kind of situation that could exist there – how the people in that church, looking back to the days of that wonderful ministry, would talk of the good old days; but I wonder if that same minister came back whether the congregation today would really enjoy his preaching. We profess as Christians, do we not, a great reverence for the concept of revival. But the staggering fact about revival is this, that whenever revival comes, the people who oppose it most are very often religious leaders. That is because revival is so devastating and so shattering. Not many of us really want it! We pay lip service to the idea of revival, but if it came we wouldn't touch it. Do we see what our Lord is getting at? We bow with traditional reverence to the names and memories of the past, we build their sepulchres, we make them ornate and garnish them, but if that man whose memory and ministry we profess to reverence came back to life and spoke, we would reject him!

I believe that this is a tragically possible line of failure – that of paying lip service to an idea that deep down in our hearts we do not really want. I have never experienced revival in the true sense, but I remember an old man in Edinburgh, an old elder of the church who had experienced revival, saying to us young fellows, 'You don't know what revival is,' and I replied, 'No we don't,' and he said, 'Revival is the sense of God's presence hanging over a whole city.' That was the great cry of the prophet: 'Oh that thou wouldest rend the heavens . . . that the mountains might flow down at thy presence' – not just at the preaching of the Word, but at thy presence! There is a depth, a dimension in revival, true revival, which transcends all human personality, and leaves a people awed and hushed and bowed, before a sense of God's presence. That is something we do not know, and I would suggest that that is something the Pharisee in us does not want!

Then we come to the final sin of the Pharisee. In v. 52 we find our Lord dealing with –

THE SIN OF HINDERING THE UNENLIGHTENED. I wonder what you would make of His words, 'Woe unto you, lawyers! for ye have taken away the key of knowledge: ye entered not in yourselves, and them that were entering in ye hindered.' I think the key to this lies in that final phrase, 'ye entered not in yourselves, and them that were entering in ye hindered'. I notice that our Lord assumes that there are those wanting to enter in, and that when trying to enter in they were hindered. I wonder whether it may not be that there are more people wanting to enter into the Christian experience than we are prepared to believe. For our Lord says not only are there those trying to enter in, but there are those who cannot enter in, and the reason is that the way is blocked by people who have not entered in themselves, and those are the Pharisees! 'Ye entered not in yourselves, and them that were entering in ye hindered.'

Tell me, is it not true that the biggest stumbling-block to the unbeliever is the believer? Again and again something about a Christian puts off someone who wants to become a Christian, and they say, 'Well, I don't know. If that's what it is, then I don't think I need pursue the matter any further.' It is rather a humbling and a searching question to ask ourselves, how many people can trace their conversion to faith in God and in Christ through our influence? That is the question that some people are very much concerned about but I do not think it is a question that any Christian ought to be concerned with primarily. It is only God who can answer that kind of question. In all probability the fact that I may have led a person to Christ has got very little to do with me at all, but has a great deal to do with a lot of people who have prayed for that soul, who have loved and spoken to that soul, and I have just taken them the last step that has brought them to Christ. That is no credit to me. A much more valuable question is, not how many people have I brought to Christ, but how many people have I put off! And the reason that I put them off, is because I have not entered into the will of God, the truth of God, the experience of Christ, and my life has been so unlike Jesus that they have been stumbled and hindered. They have wanted a new life, but they could not see it in me. I have often thought of that telling little phrase about Christ, 'They came to him,' and I find myself asking the question, 'How many people have ever come to me?' I may find myself chasing after them, but that is not the point. Do they ever come to me? Is there something about my way of life, my quality of life that draws them irresistibly, so that they say, 'I must find out the secret'? Hindering the unenlightened is the final sin of the Pharisee!

Well, there they are – the sins of the religious life. Let us list them again. Stressing the unimportant: has that sin gone out of the Church? I do not think so. Seeking the unmerited; concealing the unworthy; preaching the unfulfilled; reverencing the unwanted; and hindering the unenlightened. Is our testimony clouded by the sins of the Pharisee? Thank God there is pardon and cleansing. And do let us grasp this – the purpose of our Lord in unveiling this kind of area of failure is not to condemn us and not to cast us down. Surely it is His intention to make us aware of failure, so that in turn we may confess it, forsake it, and be pardoned and forgiven, and then walk entirely in the light even as He is in the light; and that we should so live a life that is pardoned and cleansed and renewed, walking in the Spirit as well as being born of the Spirit, and bearing the fruit of the Spirit. Then our gathering and our study will be worth while, and will mean His greater glory in the way we serve in the Church of His beloved Son. May it be so, for His name's sake.

17

Who is my neighbour?

'But a certain Samaritan, as he journeyed, came . . . and had compassion on him' (Luke 10. 33).

THERE IS A subtle danger to which the Christian finds himself exposed – that of thinking that the fact that he is a Christian gives him an immunity from some of the severer judgments of our Lord. All the time he fails to recognise that some of the most severe of these were made against those who, like the Christian, claimed to give God a place in their lives. The story of the Good Samaritan is one of the parables which, alas, has so suffered in the hands of preachers that the failure of the priest and the Levite are today scarcely noted. But it is this very failure that I want to think through with you. In the first place, consider how we have in this parable the picture of –

A MISERY THAT WAS UNDISPUTED. Think of *the plight of the man* who fell among thieves. We read that he was 'stripped . . . wounded . . . half dead'. The fact of human need is one that we cannot but face. But how loth we are to do just this! We are living in a world of the most appalling need. Whether the situation is viewed from the material or spiritual point of view, the moral or the physical, there are millions of men, women and children for whom life is one long tragedy of deprivation. It may be the wretchedly paid minister of the little church trying to make ends meet on a pittance of a salary; or the native women of India in the appalling suffering that so many of them know. It may be the despairing plight of the refugees in Palestine; or the spiritual darkness of the wealthy home in the next street. The fact of human need is a fact of life. There are so many who, like the man who fell among thieves, have been deprived of that which is their right, that which they need in order to live as God meant men to live.

But if we consider the plight of the man, we have also to contend with *the powers in the world*, the powers that rob, that would destroy. Those forces, like the lurking robbers of that Eastern highway, which wait to spring out and with a ruthless force take from men their true wealth. Those forces may be rooted in the religions of heathendom, or they may be covered over with all the polish and supposed culture of the western world. They may even be garbed in the dress of the Christian Church. But there is a ruthless power about them that seems irresistible. Their attack may be along the lines of financial gain like the drink trade, or along the lines of national loyalty; their impact may rob the pockets of those they get into their clutches or ruin the morals of those who come under their influence. But powers there are, and strong they are too, and how many lives today lie stripped, wounded and half-dead, ravaged and robbed!

So, in the second place, let us consider –

A Mentality that was Undisturbed. Here is the point we would like to pass by, namely that the men who failed were the religious men; but let us face it. 'There came down a certain priest that way, and when he saw him he passed by on the other side. And likewise a Levite, when he was at the place, came and looked at him, and passed by on the other side.' Think of *the importance of their position*: they were both men engaged in the service of God, who, it could be assumed, would understand the will of God, and who ought to be anxious to do that will in their lives. They were men recognised by others for what they were.

Is this not just where the Christian stands today? We, who name the name of Christ, are supposedly those who know something of the will of God and are committed to the doing of it. Whether we like it or not, we are witnesses. Christ said we should be witnesses: 'Ye shall be witnesses.' Whether bad witnesses or good witnesses, witnesses we must be. The Christian in some way stands between men and God. So many men can see God only through the Christian, for so few of them read their Bibles where they can see Him in Christ.

And then look at *the indifference of their hearts*: they 'passed by on the other side'. They didn't care, or at least didn't care enough to do anything about it. In both cases they were aware of the facts. The priest 'saw him', the Levite 'came and looked on him', but they both passed by. They knew, but they didn't care enough, these men who stood between the people and God. Is that where some of us come into the picture? We know, and in some measure we are sorry, we care – but not enough to do anything about it. We don't give anything more on a missionary Sunday than we do any other Sunday. We are not interested in the salary our minister is getting. We don't want our children to be missionaries: we would rather they got a nice comfortable job with good pay at home. We never go to the prayer-meeting: why should we, when there is such a good programme on the television? And, of course, we never ask anybody to go to church with us. We care, we are sorry, and all that sort of thing, but we don't care enough to do anything. And therefore we come right into the target area that our Lord is attacking. The condemnation of our Lord is laid right at our respectable churchgoing door. We know, but when faced with the need 'we pass by on the other side'. We don't care enough to act.

Let us look then, at the third lesson of this parable where Christ sets forth –

A MINISTRY THAT WAS UNDISMAYED. 'A certain Samaritan, as he journeyed, came where he was; and when he saw him, he had compassion on him . . .' Do we need to read the rest of the story, we know it so well? Think *how unhesitating his ministry* was. There might have been an attack on him also, but he didn't seem to worry about the possibility. He was too concerned about the man in trouble to think of himself at all. He didn't stop to think out how much money he might have to spend to resolve the situation; he got the wounded man up on to his beast and brought him to the inn. He did not seem to worry about the upsetting of his own plans, the possible delay to himself, the spoiling of the harnessing of his beast. There was a need in front of him and something he must do.

How desperately we need today this awareness of others, this attitude which sees that something needs to be done and then goes and does it! The attitude which the Master showed when He washed the disciples' feet. The attitude which does not wait to be asked, but which thinks of others first and not of itself. Yes, the ministry of that man was unhesitating; and also *how unexpected it was*, for he was a Samaritan! How the unexpected ministries of life judge, rebuke and condemn us! The people who do the work are so often the unexpected folk. How often in church life, the office-bearers are conspicuous by their absence at the prayer-meetings, the open-airs, the places where the real spiritual issues of the redemptive will of God are settled. Instead, their places are taken by the simple, the un-noticed, the un-named, the unexpected folk. Sometimes it is even more searching – it is the supposedly unconverted woman in the street who does the shopping for the sick mother, who looks after her children, who takes in a nicely cooked meal . . . while the Christian passes by on the other side. So often it is not the wealthy who give the generous gifts, the people who could afford it, but it is the folk who have least who give most. Yes, and in certain places it is not the supposedly Christian West that reflects a concern for the well-being of the nationals of some of the more backward countries, but the Communist East!

There is an opportunity facing the Church today such as we have never faced before, an opportunity of need. The responsibility of meeting that need is ours, but are we accepting it? Are you leading a burdened beast right now, or are you hurrying away from the facts you know, the need you have seen; hurrying on, comfortable and complacent – but condemned!

18

The light of the world

> 'Then spake Jesus again unto them, saying, I am the light of the world: he that followeth me shall not walk in darkness but shall have the light of life' (John 8. 12).

SOME YEARS AGO Dr. Paul Rees, to whose ministry I owe an immense debt, gave a series of Bible Readings at the great Christian Holiday Crusade held at Filey, on the sayings of Jesus introduced by the words 'I am' – 'I am the way', 'I am the bread of life', etc. That series was titled 'How Jesus introduced Himself', and among the studies inevitably there was one on this text, 'I am the light of the world'. Reading the book that was published containing these addresses I found myself impressed by Dr. Rees' sub-title, which ran thus, 'These are words in which we see that Christ is what we mean by splendour', and he adds, 'everything in life, no matter how glamorous, how decorative we try to make it, is paltry, cheap and tawdry if Jesus Christ's glory is not there'. 'I am the light of the world: he that followeth me shall not walk in darkness, but shall have the light of life.'

I want to try and catch again something of the splendour that shines and flashes from these wonderful words as we hold them in our hands. I want to bring you words of assurance; a word of assurance to all who maybe have committed their lives to Christ and who are wondering a little bit fearfully what it is all going to mean, and maybe specially a word of assurance to those who are still hesitating to take the step of commitment to Christ that God has been calling them to take. Well, here is a word from Christ Himself, that will, I believe, allay all fears — it is a word full of hope. I want, then, to note first of all what I have called —

THE SUPREMACY THAT CHRIST CLAIMS. 'I am the light of the World.' What a staggering claim for any man to make! Either the One who made it was mad or He was God! Of what does this claim speak, then? I want to suggest that it tells us that in Christ we face *a splendour that will excel.* There are degrees of splendour, degrees of light, degrees of brilliance; but Christ claims here a splendour that excels all others. 'I am *the* light of the world.' Whether we are thinking in terms of light as divine truth or moral excellence, here is a splendour that excels all others. In practical terms it will mean that if we commit ourselves to this One who is the light of the world, that our whole pattern of living will be changed not simply for the better, but for the best. A man may be a good man, but in Christ he will be an infinitely better man if the light of Christ's presence illumines his being. A home may be a good home, but it will be an infinitely better home if it is a truly Christian home of which it could be said that Christ is the Head of the house. A nurse may be a good nurse, but she will be an infinitely better nurse if she is a Christian nurse. A boss may be a good boss, but an infinitely better one if he is a Christian. A worker may be a good worker, but he will be a better worker if he is a Christian: and so we could go on. You and I may think some things are splendid, but as the light of a candle pales before the coming of the dawn light of the sun, so all that is good pales before the splendour that is in Jesus Christ. There is in Christ a splendour that will excel. I remember somebody saying that they had met many people who seemed perfectly happy and yet they were not Christians, to which the reply was made, 'Their happiness is like that of a blind man who has never seen!' Think of the happiness of a blind person who has never seen, and then think of the splendour of some of the sunsets that you have seen, and think how much the blind person has missed! A splendour that will excel – this is what we find in Christ!

And closely linked in with that we find here *a splendour that will expose*. You may recall the words of Christ, 'light has come into the world', He says, concerning Himself, 'and men have loved darkness rather than light, because their deeds are evil'. Light reveals, light exposes what would otherwise remain unseen. Why is it that when the brighter light of springtime and early summer comes, the ladies get busy purchasing their spring and early summer outfits? Simply because the dull days of the winter have concealed the fact that their other clothes were beginning to get shabby, but when the brighter light comes and they see the shabbiness they had not seen before, to their husbands' dismay they want to buy new outfits! They want something that is fresh, something that is lovely, something that is good, something that is gay, because the light has come and exposed the shabbiness. It is that way with Christ. Christ says, 'If I had not come they had not had sin; but now they have no cloke for their sin.' And when the dazzling splendour and glory, truth and excellence shines out from the person of Christ and we are caught in the full glare of its brilliance, we see things in our lives we never saw before. We are shown up for what we are. As long as we compare ourselves with our neighbours, or with other folk in the church, we think we are doing not too badly; but when we are brought into the glare and the dazzling light of Jesus Christ we see that we are sinners, dreadful sinners, and the reaction to that experience is all important. Are we going to run away from it and delude ourselves into thinking we are all right, or are we going to remain in the light so that we might face up to the facts as they are? We do so like to think that we are all right, and it is shattering to find that we are not!

Here we have found a splendour that will excel, and a splendour that will expose. Does this help us to explain the strange paradox that we find in Christian biography, that the longer Christians remain in the light, the farther they travel in Christian experience and the nearer they get to the light, so the opinions they hold of themselves get lower and lower. The greatest saints will see themselves to be the greatest sinners. More and more they realise they are not what they should be. The more that they are exposed to the light, the closer they get to its brilliance, the more they see themselves as they really are. The greatest of saints are not filled with a sense of their goodness but with a sense of their unworthiness.

I recall an incident that was told me of something that happened at the great Keswick Convention, held annually in the English Lake District. A remarkable meeting had taken place in the huge marquee seating five thousand people in which God had used one of His servants mightily and the great congregation had been hushed and stilled under an awesome sense of the presence of God, and the congregation had dispersed in utter silence. Some time after the meeting, the person who was telling me of this said that he had returned to the speakers' house, and was walking along the corridor to his room when he was suddenly arrested by sounds of great distress coming from behind a door that he was passing. He stopped, wondering what was the matter; who it was; whether he should knock and go in. The sounds of distress and sobbing and weeping went on unabated, and finally he knocked at the door gently and opened it, and there he found to his utter amazement the very man who had been so greatly used of God in that great convention, bowed at his bedside, weeping as if his heart would break! He was completely overwhelmed with a sense of his utter unworthiness. In Christ there is a splendour that will expose. If you think that being a Christian is going to turn you into a religious Jack Horner, that you are going to sit in your corner and take out your Christmas pie and put in your thumb and pull out a plum and say, 'What a good boy am I,' I tell you this, that the nearer you get to the light the more you will see your sin. Here there is the supremacy that Christ claims: 'I am *the* light of the world'; a splendour that will excel all others, and a splendour that will expose all sins.

Then we come to the next fantastic statement. 'I am the light of the world,' says Christ, 'he that followeth me . . .' A supremacy that Christ claims, and —

A PROXIMITY THAT CHRIST SEEKS. 'He that followeth me,' and the jump in thought is, as Dr. Rees points out, from a planet to a person. 'I am the light of the world: he that followeth me . . .' And yet the jump is inevitable, for the world is what the individuals make it, and Christ's concern is for the individual and the relationship that He wants is described here in the words 'He that followeth me'.

There are two aspects of this relationship that to me are wonderful: first there is *the intimacy that Christ wants us to enjoy.* The 'following' is surely meant to describe a relationship of closeness, of nearness, of fellowship, of intimacy; not following at a distance! It is a 'following' close behind, indicative of that characteristic of love in which we see that love is never content to remain at a distance, that loves craves for contact, for nearness, to be so near that it may share the experiences and the thoughts, share the joys and share the sorrows, the injuries and the triumphs. Human love is never content to remain at a distance, and God's love is not content to remain at a distance. 'He that followeth me.'

What parent but knows this longing to be near the child ill in hospital! Just to be there, to know, to share! What sweetheart separated from a lover, but longs for contact, for nearness! My church in Glasgow on a Sunday night used to be filled with young folk sitting in the gallery – I was thrilled to see them there in their hundreds; and I know pretty well, although I have no evidence to support it, that when I used to see fellows and girls sitting close together and sharing a hymn-book that, when I was preaching the sermon, in all probability they would be holding hands! Love wants to be near, love wants contact, and the fantastic thing is that the One who says 'I am the light of the world' wants us. He wants you, He wants me, so that He can share with us. Do you remember the words of Christ in John 14, 'If a man love me ... my Father will love him, and we will come to him, and make our abode with him.' 'He that loveth me shall be loved of my Father, and I will love him, and will manifest myself to him.' Here is the unfolding of love's deepest thought in fellowship; a sharing! And this is the incredible light that you and I are called into, so that God in Christ can share with us. His thoughts. An intimacy that Christ wants us to enjoy. This Saviour of ours, this Son of God, is wanting our company, to share His thoughts; his longing for our responsive trust. 'He that followeth me', this is what the Christian life is all about. Not a whole lot of taboos and traditions that evangelicalism has brought out – thou shalt not ... thou shalt not ... thou shalt not. The living heart of the business is companying with Jesus Christ. You companying with Him and He with you.

The proximity that Christ seeks: 'I am the light of the world: he that followeth me.' The intimacy that Christ wants us to enjoy, and *the authority that Christ asks us to obey*: for to follow is to obey. All of us must surely have played 'follow my leader' when we were children, a simple enough game – whatever the leader does, the rest do; wherever the leader goes, the rest go. And following Him speaks of not only an intimacy to be enjoyed but an authority to be obeyed. Some of us have so reacted away from Christ as an example and from the law that we have overlooked the fact that Christ is just exactly that – He is an example. 'If I your

Master and Lord have ...' He says, 'so you ought also.' 'A new commandment I give you, that ye love one another as I have loved you.' Christ as an example; Christ as a Master; the Lordship of Christ – these are the truths that run right through the New Testament. Paul writes of Him as the One who is the Head of the Church, that in all things He might have pre-eminence. The Christian is someone whose life has passed under new management, so that following Him means the acceptance of His authority in our lives. The final beatitude recorded in Scripture states, 'Blessed are they that do His commandments', and that is in the last chapter of the Bible. In our obedience is found the purpose of our redemption by God, the proof of our devotion to God, the pathway to our experience of God; and 'he that followeth me' speaks not only of an intimacy that He wants me to enjoy, but an authority He asks me to obey.

The supremacy that Christ claims; the proximity that Christ seeks; and finally –

THE SECURITY THAT CHRIST GIVES. 'I am the light of the world: he that followeth me ...' What? 'shall not walk in darkness, but shall have (in himself) the light of life.' The security that Christ gives. And there are two thoughts here with which we must close. First, *the avoidance of the perils that can destroy a life*, the perils that darkness conceals. In John 11. 10 Christ says, 'If a man walk in the night, he stumbleth.' What happens if people are stumbling in the darkness of ignorance or in the darkness of sin, or the darkness of this world? What happens if people are stumbling about in the dark? Well, they get lost in the dark. Do you know folk who have got hopelessly lost? I remember when I was in Cockfosters, after the first Billy Graham crusade I was asked by the BBC to interview various people who had been converted at Harringay. All sorts of people from every walk of life who had been converted in every kind of circumstance. Amongst them was a young actor, and I said to him,

'Well, I am very interested and in a sense a little bit surprised to meet you.' I added, 'As far as young people generally are concerned, they assume that once you get your name in the lights and you are getting to the top of the world of the theatre or the films, that life is one gay round. It is surprising to hear you talk of finding something at Harringay that you hadn't found.' I asked, 'Are the people in your world, your strata of society, not extremely happy people?' I have never forgotten his reply. 'Happy!' he said: 'in my world of the theatre and the film industry you will find attempts at happiness, pretence of happiness, but real happiness – no!' And how tragically often we read in the Press that men and women, young and old from that strata of society have committed suicide. People who have got lost, utterly lost. They just cannot find the way. They don't know where to find happiness; they don't know where to find peace; they don't know where to find a way out of their problems; they don't know how to find a way through. A man who came to see me in my vicarage in London said, 'You will be surprised to see me' – and I was, for he never came to church. He was a lecturer in psychology, and psychology was the be-all and the end-all and the cure-all. He said, 'I have come to see you, Mr. Duncan – you will be surprised to see me – but my marriage is in ruins.' He was lost, in the dark!

People get hurt in the dark. Have you ever hurt yourself in the dark? You tripped over something you didn't see. You fell; you hurt yourself. How many people get hurt in the dark? And they not only get hurt themselves, they hurt other folk. I wonder if there is someone reading these words who is living without Christ. Your children are getting hurt by you. If ever I felt like putting my foot through a television screen it is when I have seen an advertisement for alcohol. When I think that alcohol can do in a home, turning homes into hells! How on earth some wives stick to their husbands through the sheer hell of having an alcoholic husband, I don't know. And what of the kids that suffer? God only knows! And all that is happening because a man is walking in the dark. Tell me, do you know a lot of folk who have got lost; who have got hurt because they are lost? Others are lost who are following them, and they are not only hurting themselves, they are hurting those that are nearest and dearest to them. Jesus says, 'I am the light of the world: he that followeth me shall not walk in darkness.' You won't be conned into thinking that happiness is to be found where it isn't; you will see because you are not in the dark, you are in the light. The avoidance of the perils that can destroy a life – 'shall not walk in darkness'. Thank God for that.

Finally, *the assurance of the presence that will direct a life.* '. . . but shall have in himself the light of life.' A light upon the pathway he should take; a light upon the perils that he should shun; a light upon the Saviour who can help and bless. Walking in the light, not stumbling in the dark. Walking with confidence; walking with assurance; walking with insight; walking with understanding. The Christian moves confidently through life until the final shadow appears, and even then at evening time for him it shall be light. This is the Christ we preach, and this is the light to which He calls. 'He that followeth me shall not walk in darkness but shall have in himself the light of life.' What a fantastic, what a wonderful way to live. What an incredible folly to turn it down. What madness to hesitate even for a moment. What a thrill to receive such a Saviour, and live such a life! The choice is ours.

19

Christ's second coming

'This same Jesus ... shall so come in like manner as ye have seen Him go' (Acts I. II).

THIS BLESSED HOPE lies at the very heart of our Christian faith. Every Christian holds this truth in his heart, and it shines like a solitary star in the gathering clouds of darkness and storm that seem to fill the horizon. This is not a truth or a belief that is the prerogative of religious cranks. This is something which is part of what we would call the catholic or universal faith of the Christian Church. There is not a creed of the catholic Church in which this hope is not expressed. There is not a hymn-book in Christendom where it is not sung, and those of us who may belong to the Church of England will know that in the liturgy of our worship, in our prayers and in our canticles, and every time we gather around the Lord's Table, we are reminded that this is part of the faith of the Christian Church.

I want to turn to some words of Christ concerning His second advent. Jesus said, 'As it was in the days of Noah ... as it was in the days of Lot ... even thus shall it be in the day when the Son of man is revealed.' Let us look, then, at those two events. It is significant that our Lord has linked the truth of His second coming with the two great judgments of the Old Testament. That gives us a principle concerning this hope of our Lord's return and it is this: that –

GOD'S JUDGMENT IS DETERMINED. In Gen. 6. 5–7, we see how man's disobedience brought the judgment of God upon men. 'God saw the wickedness of man was great in the earth, and every imagination of the thoughts of his heart only evil continually ... and it grieved Him ... And the Lord said, I will destroy him whom I have created from the face of the earth.' How terrible the corruption of life must have been we can gather from the drastic nature of God's action. There had been such a corruption of the physical system of life between man created in God's image and some lower or higher form of life, that the only way to save the human race was to destroy the evil. But the point is that at that hour, judgment was determined. When we turn to Gen. 18, 'As it was in the days of Lot,' we read that it was the same. 'Their sin is very grievous,' and we find God moving into action – the action of judgment.

What of the day of Christ's return? 'As it was ... so shall it be.' Of the sin and unbelief in the world today there can be no doubt, and sometimes when people complain that God does not seem to be doing very much, they forget that God speaks of a time when He will act. 'The Lord Jesus shall be revealed from heaven with his mighty angels, in flaming fire taking vengeance on them that know not God.' And nothing is clearer from the Word of God than that history is moving steadily towards the great final crisis of judgment. 'We believe that thou shalt come.' For what? 'To be our judge.' Judgment is determined.

The second 'as it was so shall it be' is that –

GOD'S MERCY WAS DECLARED. Nowhere in the Bible do you find judgment without mercy. Mercy was declared in the days of Noah. We read in 2 Peter 2. 5 that Noah was 'a preacher of righteousness'. He declared God's mercy. During the years when the ark was being built, the message of judgment and mercy was heralded forth. In the days of Lot, 'then came the angels ... to bring them out of this place', and God's mercy again was declared. So too it shall be in the day when our Lord returns. It will be a day, He himself has told us, 'when this gospel of the kingdom shall be preached in all the world for a witness, and then shall the end come'. There are parts of the earth where the message of the Gospel has not been heralded and the name of Jesus Christ has not been heard, but we are told that the Gospel shall be preached in all the world for a witness. Judgment is always bound up with mercy, and the God who judges is a God who would save.

Thirdly, we note how –

GOD'S MESSAGE WAS DESPISED. In the days of the flood, only eight persons responded. Only eight entered the ark, and one can imagine the scorn and ridicule that would greet the sermon as Noah went from village to village. What does the high-born lady of society think of this; or the man at the factory bench, whose chief interest in life is to fill up his football coupon? What does this mean to them? Absolutely nothing, I am afraid. And yet 'as it was, so shall it be'. What about the days of Lot? Was the message proclaimed then received with gladness? 'Lot went out and spoke unto his sons-in-law, and said, Get you out of this place ... but he seemed to them as one that mocked.' I read in 2 Peter 3. 3, 'Knowing this first, that there shall come in the last days scoffers, walking after their own lusts and saying, Where is the promise of His coming?' There are many people who do not believe in judgment. They do not believe there is anything to escape from. If they believe in the after-life at all, they do not believe in this kind of after-life. And so God's message is despised.

What else happened then and will happen when He comes? –

GOD'S PEOPLE WERE DELIVERED. In the days of the flood, before the judgment fell, those who had believed God's word were taken into safety. 'Noah went in, and his sons, and his wife, and sons' wives with him, into the ark.' In the days of Lot we see a small band of people hurrying out of the city. The Lord was merciful to them and brought them forth; and so shall it be. 'Then shall two be in the field: the one shall be taken, and the other left.' 'For this we say unto you by the word of the Lord, that we which are alive and remain unto the coming of the Lord shall not prevent them which are asleep, for the Lord himself shall descend from heaven with a shout, with the voice of the archangel and with the trump of God; and the dead in Christ shall rise first: then we which are alive and remain shall be caught up together with them in the clouds, to meet the Lord in the air; and so shall we ever be with the Lord.' God's people were delivered then, and as it was so shall it be. And –

GOD'S ENEMIES WERE DOOMED. Gen. 7. 23, 'Every living thing was destroyed.' Gen. 19. 24, 'Then the Lord rained upon Sodom and Gomorrah brimstone and fire.' The smoke went up as the smoke of a furnace. So shall it be: 'Behold, he cometh with clouds; and every eye shall see him, and they also which pierced him: and all kindreds of the earth shall wail because of him.' In his book, *The Lord's Coming*, Dr. Graham Scroggie speaks of the astronomer Kepler studying the mystery of the heavens, trying to discover the laws governing the movement of the planets, and finding that they eluded his grasp. He had been experimenting on his theory that they moved around one focus, and every time he saw them coming into the heavens the mystery remained unsolved till suddenly it dawned upon him that they were not moving around one focus but two foci; and when he applied this theory, the heavens yielded up the mystery that had baffled him for so long; then rising up from his study he said, 'O God, I am thinking thy thoughts after thee.'

The Christian who is thinking in terms of one coming will never understand God's scheme of history and redemption. God's mind is not moving around one coming. 'One coming first in humility,' to quote the Prayer Book, but then 'the second coming in majesty and glory'. 'As it was, so shall it be.'

20

The ministry of grateful love

'Then took Mary a pound of ointment of spikenard, very costly, and anointed the feet of Jesus' (John 12. 3).

ONE OF THE choicest of all characters found in the New Testament records of the life and ministry of Jesus Christ, is surely that of Mary of Bethany. Visitors to the Holy Land will almost certainly visit Bethany and the beautiful church that has been built on the traditional site of this home where Jesus loved to go. In that simple church there are the most exquisitely beautiful mosaics depicting the occasions in which Mary met with the Lord she loved. Possibly one of the choicest of all incidents took place, not in her own home, but in the nearby home of Simon. If ever a person loved Christ, Mary did, and it would do us all good to measure the love we profess for our Lord and Saviour against the love so evidently displayed by Mary.

A great preacher once said that 'while faith makes all things possible, love makes all things easy', and most of our problems in our lives as individuals and in the corporate life of our church fellowships would be resolved if we loved our Lord more truly and more deeply. Dr. S. D. Gordon, a well-

known preacher from America in a former generation, has
described how love is the secret of all true Christian character and life. He writes, 'Peace is love resting, prayer is love
keeping tryst, enthusiasm is love burning, sympathy is
love tenderly feeling, hope is love expecting, patience is love
waiting, faithfulness is love holding fast, humility is love
taking its true place, modesty is love keeping out of sight,
soul winning is love pleading.' I remember reading of an
incident in the story of the Salvation Army when some
missionaries in India were so discouraged in their work that
they wrote to General William Booth and asked if they
might be re-allocated to a less exacting sphere of service.
The General sent them a curt cable containing just two
words: 'Try love'. And this of course is the secret of it all. We
discovered this when our children were small. One of our
sons started to learn to play the piano; he didn't like it, and
to get him to practise was always a battle. Then one day by
chance, it might seem, he got his hands on the church organ,
and immediately everything was different; he loved playing
the organ although he didn't love playing the piano at that
time. We discovered that while it had been difficult to get
him to practise for a very short time on the piano, now it was
as difficult to get him to leave the organ! The difference was
a simple one: he loved the organ but not the piano.

So let us take a look at the love Mary of Bethany demonstrated for her Lord in the choice incident recorded in John
12. 1-11, and in doing so let us remember that Christian love
is something that the Christian receives when he receives the
new life. When Christ comes to dwell in our hearts by His
Spirit He brings not only His life but His love with it. So we
read in Rom. 5. 5, 'The love of God has been shed abroad in
our hearts by the Holy Spirit who has been given to us.'

Concerning this exquisite scene in Bethany, I want us to
note –

THE QUALITY THAT MARKS THE MINISTRY OF LOVE: and

there are two qualities. First, I can see here *the extravagance of love*. We read, 'Then took Mary a pound of ointment of spikenard, *very costly*, and anointed the feet of Jesus.' I have never forgotten the impact made upon my mind when reading this passage many years ago. I suddenly noticed the words 'very costly'. They seemed to stand out as if written in pure gold – 'very costly'. We see the sheer extravagance of love's giving. And is this not true about love in human relationships? Love is extravagant in the price it is willing to pay. The gift for the sweetheart will not be the cheapest but the dearest that love can afford. The holiday for the family will in all probability cost more than was originally intended. The clothes for the children will be the best that money can buy; the birthday present for husband or wife will never be the cheapest but the dearest! There is an extravagance about the price that love is willing to pay; indeed, love is not only willing to pay such a price, but love demands such a price. Do you remember the words spoken by David in 2 Sam. 24. 24, when he was given the chance of getting something cheaply for God? David replied almost with contempt, 'Neither will I offer to the Lord my God that which doth cost me nothing.'

There will also be an extravagance about the time that love is willing to give – time to listen; time to be with the one loved. Love never thinks in terms of the minimum, but always in terms of the maximum; and love will give its time without grudging a minute of it. Why, even if two lovers are saying just two words to each other, 'good night', they seem to take about thirty minutes to say them! Yet I remember someone once saying to me that he loved his church, but as he scarcely ever darkened its doors and seemed to give no time to it, I found that statement difficult to believe. How many Christians there are who seem to think they do well if they give to the God they profess to love one-and-a-half hours out of their time in every week!

There will also be an extravagance about the strength that

love is willing to spend. Think of the unending, unremitting expenditure of strength that a mother's love accepts without complaint. I sometimes think that a mother's work is the hardest, the most exacting, the most exhausting work, and yet it is all done without grudging and without complaint. The extravagance of love. The price that love is willing to pay, the time that love is willing to give, the strength that love is willing to spend. I wonder how far our love that we take so readily for granted comes up to the standard of Mary's love.

But there is another aspect of the quality that marked the ministry of Mary's love as as we see it in Bethany, and that I have called *the fragrance of love*. We read, 'The house was filled with the fragrance of the ointment.' Not only was there a lavishness about the ministry of Mary's love but there was a loveliness about it too! There was a fragrance, something attractive, something arresting, something compelling, something that gave deep pleasure. Tell me, are there fragrant memories in your life? Memories that send a warm glow through your heart, that will bring a smile to your face and light to your eyes? If there are such memories, I am sure that more often than not there will be love somewhere in them – maybe the love of our earthly parents, or maybe the love of our heavenly Father! Certain places will always be lovely, and our memories of them fragrant, because when we were there we lived in the glow and in the warmth of human love – the place that was home, the places where our holidays were spent. In my own life our summer holidays were so often spent in the villages of Speyside in the Scottish Highlands, and the very names of these villages bring back lovely memories – Nethy Bridge, Carrbridge, Dulnain Bridge, Aviemore, Newtonmore, Grantown, Cromdale; and so I could go on! There will always be a fragrance about the names of places like that!

So too in our memories of people, their very names, the very sound of their voices, warm us, simply because of the love they showed towards us, the way they thought about us and were concerned for us. In my church in Glasgow our choir used to sing an anthem that was a great favourite of mine. It began with the words, 'Jesus, Jesus, Jesus, there is something about that name!' What about our names, what about the places that people associate with us, is there a fragrance created in their minds when they think of us? Do you recall the words of St. Paul in 2 Cor. 2. 14, 'Thanks be to God, who leads us wherever we are on his own triumphant way, and makes our knowledge of him to spread throughout the world like a lovely perfume. We Christians have the unmistakable fragrance of Christ' – a lovely perfume and an unmistakable fragrance! Is that office a lovelier place because you work in it; that home, that school, that hospital ward? I remember hearing of a Christian nurse who had been off duty, and when she came back to go on night duty she went into a private ward where an old lady lay very sick and very weary. She turned her head to see who had come in, and when she saw who it was she said, 'I am so glad it is you!' Are people glad when we are with them, or do they wish we weren't there? I think it is Rita Snowden who in one of her books recalls an incident in her life when she was on holiday in Devon or Cornwall. She was sitting at the window when suddenly the air seemed to fill with perfume and fragrance. She wondered where it came from, and her curiosity was aroused. She went out into the road, but she could see nothing unusual except that a lot of people seemed to be passing by. She asked one of them where this fragrance came from, and the person said, 'Oh, that's quite simply explained, we work in a perfume factory, and are going home for lunch!' The quality that marks the ministry of love, the extravagance of it, and the fragrance of it!

We also have what I have called –

THE SYMPATHY THAT GUIDES THE MINISTRY OF LOVE. We can sense two facets of this aspect of true love, and the first is *the wisdom that it reveals.* They say that love is blind, and it may be blind to faults, but it is not blind to thoughts! As far as thoughts go, love is the very opposite of blind: there is a discernment, an insight about love that sees beneath the outward appearances. This is what Paul prayed for for the Christians at Philippi. He prayed that they might have a love that was 'full of knowledge and wise insight', an insight born out of that knowledge. This was a social occasion in Bethany, it was a time for thanksgiving, Lazarus had been raised from the dead, and everyone it seemed was in a joyous mood! No, not everyone: two people were not rejoicing; they were thoughtful rather. Jesus was one, and Mary was the other. The thoughts of Jesus Christ were elsewhere, and Mary knew, and she knew because she loved. Love not only gives, love knows. The cross was just round the corner, and the shadow of it lay dark and heavy across the mind of Christ. It was Dr. Graham Scroggie who said, 'There is so much awkward piety, so much blundering goodness, so much unattractive sanctity.' What a tragic indictment that is, 'blundering goodness, awkward piety, unattractive sanctity'. We lack the insight and the wisdom because we lack the love, and we lack the love because we lack the knowledge – the wisdom it reveals.

And also we can see here *the welcome it receives.* To give such a ministry, and above all to get it, is something beyond the price of rubies. How grateful Jesus Christ was for Mary's loving ministry. You recall how the cold, critical, calculating voice of Judas broke in – and there is almost always a Judas in the company of the disciples of the Lord. He spoke harshly, 'Why was not this ointment sold for three hundred pence, and given to the poor?' Swiftly and sharply came the retort of Christ, almost with a glint of cold steel in His voice, 'Leave her alone!' As if our Lord was saying, 'Judas, you are out of this altogether; you have no part or lot in what's happening here; you just don't belong, and don't you dare rob me of this kind of understanding. Mary knows what none of you have the sense or the love to know. Against the day of my burying hath she kept this.' But Mary had brought it at that moment; Mary in her love and wisdom knew what was awaiting Christ, and she wanted Him to know that she at least knew and cared and loved! The welcome such a ministry receives – how grateful Jesus Christ was!

We sometimes might do well to ask if people are grateful when we are around; are they thankful to see us, are they glad to have us in their company? This sympathy that guides the ministry of love is shown so clearly in Mary, the wisdom it reveals and the welcome it receives. We have noted, then, the quality that marks the ministry of love, the sympathy that quides the ministry of love. There is one more thing that we can see here that is worth noting; it is what I have called –

THE MEMORY THAT CROWNS THE MINISTRY OF LOVE. In St. Mark's account and St. Matthew's account we are told that Jesus said, 'Wheresoever this Gospel shall be preached throughout the whole world, this also that she hath done shall be spoken of for a memorial of her.' The memory that crowns the ministry of love is, first of all, *an enduring memory*. Christ said, 'As long as, and wherever the Gospel is preached, the memory of Mary's love and ministry will remain fresh and living.' Love gives, we know that; love knows, we know that; and love lasts, we know that! In the life of a family, in the life of a church, the memories that linger are the memories of those who loved, who cared! Someone has said that 'everyone needs someone to love and someone to be loved by', and where there is demonstrated this unselfish concern for others, being in itself the evidence of the validity of their love, that life will be remembered not because of the position or office held in the church, not because of the work done, but because of the love they showed – an enduring memory.

And *an enriching memory* too! What a summons is here, what a challenge is here! All down the years Christians have sensed the call to a truer, deeper, stronger love as they have witnessed Mary's love for her Lord, and the life of the Church has been enriched as Christians have sought to reach the standard set in this Bethany home all those years ago. What kind of memory will people have of you and of me? We may have been office bearers in our churches, members of the choir, teachers in the Sunday-schools, but how will we be remembered? What associations will the recollection of your name and mine conjure up in the memories of others? Will there be a fragrance about our name? It was Robert Murray McCheyne who said, 'Live so as to be missed!' Will you be missed, will I? There are two poems and a prayer with which I would like to end; they all mean much to me. Here is the first poem: I forget where it came from, but the words mean such a lot —

> Love ever gives,
> Forgives, outlives, and ever stands
> With open hands;
> And while it lives it gives,
> For this is love's prerogative:
> To give, and give, and give.

And here is the second poem. It is entitled, 'The fruit of the Spirit is love' —

> Joy is love exulting, and peace is love at rest,
> Patience love enduring in every trial and test;
> Gentleness, love yielding to all that is not sin,
> Goodness, love in action that flows from Christ within;
> Faith is love's eyes opened the living Christ to see;
> Meekness, love not fighting but bowed at Calvary;
> Temperance is love in harness and under Christ's control:
> For Christ is love in person; and love, Christ in the soul.

And here is the prayer – an old, old prayer; but what a prayer to pray! 'O divine Master, grant that I may not so much seek to be consoled as to console, to be understood as to understand, to be loved as to love; for it is in giving that we receive, it is in pardoning that we are pardoned, it is in dying that we are born to eternal life.'

Remember, then, that while faith makes all things possible, love makes all things easy!

21

Rivers of living water

'Jesus stood and cried, saying, If any man thirst, let him come unto me and drink. He that believeth on me, as the Scripture hath said, out of his innermost being shall flow rivers of living water' (John 7. 37–39).

ONE OF OUR modern translations adds to this text the challenging and significant word, 'continually'. I want to try to conjure something of the astounding picture that our Lord reveals to us in these wonderful words, concerning the ultimate pattern and portrayal of what the Christian life is really meant to be. Out of our innermost being there are to flow continually rivers of living water. Have you and I come in any measure of understanding and experience, within sight of this amazing purpose of God? First let us note –

HOW ARRESTING IS THE OFFER. 'If any man . . .' So this objective, this target, this portrayal of the life that is indwelt by the Holy Spirit, as a life out of which are flowing rivers of living water continually, *is inclusive of all*: this is for '*any man*'! This is for the housewife washing the nappies of the baby in the home, or the girl hammering the keys of her typewriter in the office, the nurse walking up the ward, the business man behind his desk, the student at university, the scholar at school, or the child in the home: this is for '*any man*'. How often, when we read some of the really staggering statements of Scripture, we say, 'Well, of course, that is not for me,' and we think of great evangelists; we think of speakers whose understanding of the Word of God far exceeds our own, and we say, 'It is for them.' But God's thoughts are not our thoughts: Christ says this experience is for 'any man'. That is the arresting thing about this offer. This is for you; this is God's intention for you where you are, and for me where I am, namely that out of our inner being there shall flow continually 'rivers of living water'. This is an offer which is arresting because it is inclusive of all. So you and I are right in the centre of this. This is what God has planned for your life and mine, by virtue of the indwelling Spirit of God. Is your life anything like that just now? Is mine?

But how arresting the offer is, not only because it is inclusive of all, but because it is *exclusive of some*. It is not simply a statement, 'If any man ...' without conditions attached. It is, 'If any man thirst, let him *come unto me and drink*.' So it is arresting because it is exclusive of some. There are some who do not qualify for this; and they do not qualify because they do not thirst, nor do they come to Christ, nor do they drink! So that is arresting, too; and I have to check up and ask myself, am I in the category of those who thirst; am I in the category of those who come to Christ and drink? What is thirst? I think it would be true to say that thirst is the most intense form of desire. In this country we are seldom thirsty. We have a little too much water, whether it is falling or flowing! We really do not know what it is to be thirsty. Oh, sometimes we say, 'I'm dying for a cup of tea,' but we are not really dying, are we? But there are countries where men and women do die of thirst.

Thirst is the most intense form of desire, and speaks here of a spiritual desire – a desire for holiness, a desire for likeness to Christ, a desire for forgiveness, a desire for life abundant, a desire for power, a desire for freedom and liberty. I remember a question I read of somewhere which challenged me: it read, 'What is the intensity of your desire?' Well, I do not know what it is, but I know where I can measure it. Our Lord has linked prayer with desire. He speaks thus, 'Whatsoever things ye desire when ye pray . . .' So if I want to know what is the intensity of someone's desire, then I have to look into the intensity of their prayers. But one of the tragic things is that if we measure the intensity of our desires by the intensity of our prayers, we find that there is very little intensity anywhere! 'If any man thirst . . .! Then what God has to offer is not for triflers. 'Blessed are they that hunger and thirst after righteousness, for they shall be filled.' I wonder how far there is a restlessness, there is almost a sense of torment in our praying? Are we among those who desire?

And our Lord does not only say, 'If any man thirst, then let him come unto me and drink . . .' I recall hearing Bishop Taylor Smith praying, and his prayer was that we might become recipients in order that we might then become donors. For if this amazing offer is inclusive of all, and yet is exclusive of some, it is exclusive of those who do not desire, it is exclusive of those who do not come to Christ and who do not drink, of those who have not really learned the secret of receiving Christ as Saviour and Christ as their very life, Christ as their Lord and Master. 'If any man thirst, let him come unto me, and drink.'

So there is an offer that is arresting: 'Out of his inner being shall flow rivers of living water.' Now let us note –

How Abounding is the Supply. Note *the dimension in which our Lord is thinking.* He is thinking in terms of rivers. I remember hearing Dr. S. D. Gordon say on one occasion, that so many Christians, far from being like rivers that are

flowing continually, are like taps that drip occasionally!
That is far too true. You may may have gone to a tap without knowing that the workmen were busy and had turned it
off at the main; you turned the tap on, and thought you
were going to get a lovely flow of sparkling, cool water, but
you just got a dribble or two and then it stopped. Is not that
what so many Christians are like? You get a wee bit of a
dribble now and again; but rivers flowing continually? –
nothing of that! Yet that is God's intention, that is what God
is aiming at, that is His target, that is His design for any
man, for any Christian. We all should be living a life on this
dimensional level. Out of our inner being then should be
flowing continually rivers of living water.

It was at the Feast of Tabernacles that our Lord was
speaking. I think that what He was really saying in terms of
living water, was in contrast to the sound with which the
worshippers at the feast were familiar – the splash of the
water poured out in the ceremony and ritual of the feast. For
seven days processions had carried water in golden vessels, to
pour it out in the temple. The significance was both historic
and prophetic; historic, in its reminder of the way in which
in the wilderness wanderings God had supplied miraculously
the water to quench their physical thirst; prophetic, in that
it looked forward to the day in which their spiritual thirst
would be quenched. On the last day there was no procession,
there was no water, indicating that as a matter of history the
wilderness wanderings had ended, and that the prophecy
had not yet been fulfilled. And into that silence and into that
gap Christ stepped, saying. 'If any man thirst, let him come
unto me, and drink. He that believeth on me, as the Scripture hath said, out of his inner being there shall flow rivers of
living water.' The rivers were to be in contrast to just the
splash and the silence. Here is something better than the
splash of water on the stone floor of the temple. Here is
something better than the drip of water from a tap. Here are

rivers of living water. To use a phrase that is common north of the border, this is a river 'in spate'. Are you living in that dimension?

We have noted the dimension in which the Lord was thinking. Now let us consider *the direction in which the rivers were flowing*: 'out of his inner being . . .' Note how Christ reverses the direction of thought. We do receive, we must receive, we go on receiving – but not in order that we may keep; rather in order that we may give. How right the Bishop was – 'recipients in order that we may become donors'. The analogy and metaphor of the Christian is not a sponge but a spring. Do you know Christians who are like sponges? 'Oh,' they say, 'I love the Gospel.' And bless their hearts, they go Sunday after Sunday, and they sit like big wet sponges in their pews. They sop it all up. They need to be squeezed! Oh, it is not a sponge, it is a spring, it is a river: out of – out of!

How arresting the offer, how abounding the supply –

How Abiding the Result. What kind of waters are these? They are called 'living waters'. I think possibly our Lord had in mind the Scripture in Ezek. 47. 9, where we read of waters so deep that they were 'waters to swim in'. Then we get this comment, that 'everything whithersoever the river shall come, shall live'. The life that both the Old and the New Testament have in mind is spiritual life, eternal life; that you and I are to live such a life in which the Holy Spirit is ministering so freely that there will be abiding results wherever we live, wherever we go. Living water – everything whithersoever the river will come, shall live.

Oh, *the difference that water makes*! In this country we do not easily appreciate it. We are not often far from the sight and sound of running water. But in other lands it is not so. Upon the coming of the rains, upon the flowing of the river, life itself depends. I remember flying from Bombay to Bangalore, on my first visit back to India since childhood. I arrived in the hot season prior to the monsoon, and as we flew over miles and miles of country below, I could not see a speck of green anywhere. The whole land was burnt brown. Yet within hours of the fall of the monsoon rain, everything was transformed. Where there had been death, there was life! And it is the transforming kind of influence that the Spirit of God wants to exercise through you and through me – a life-giving influence, that will transform into life and beauty and fragrance lives that seem dead and drab. 'Out of your inner being flowing continually rivers of living water.' What difference do you make to others? Are there lives that thank God for you?

I remember once I took time to write to the man to whom under God I owe my conversion as a boy, Mr. Hudson Pope. Later I met him, and said, 'It is so lovely to see you. Do you remember the first time we met?' And he said, 'Yes; and you were twelve years old.' Rivers of living water! This was a man whose name was never in the headlines of the newspapers, and yet I wonder how many children, boys and girls, owe their eternal life, under God, to the fact that Dick Hudson Pope lived so truly under the ministry of the Holy Spirit, that out of his inner being there were continually flowing rivers of living water. What a welcome he must have got on the other side; what a crown!

Are you doing that kind of work? Are you making that kind of difference? Are you exercising this transforming ministry, in your home, where you work, in your family circle, among your relations? Is the living water bringing life?

The difference that water makes. But note finally, *the distance that water flows*. I recall a train journey from New Delhi, when I was making my way up to Mussoorie and Landour to minister to the conventions there. The train was going up a valley where, even at summer level, the water still flowed. And I noticed as I looked out of the window, how carefully the water was drawn off into one channel, and then into a smaller channel, and then into a still smaller channel, until scores and scores of fields were being irrigated far, far away from the river itself. The distance the water travels! And so it is with the rivers of living water of which Christ speaks. They will travel into this home, and into that, and into another, and from that to another. By the channel of your prayers, rivers may be flowing in Africa, or India. By your gifts the rivers may be flowing in Korea, or out in Malaya. By your words, spoken or written, the rivers can flow anywhere. Do you know, this is the most tremendous thing about the Christian life. This is the staggering thing about it, that you can be the most obscure person, holding no office in the church, your name never appearing in the parish magazine, and yet you can be counting for God all over the world. 'Out of his inner being rivers of living water flowing continually.'

May I end with a simple statement that I came across the other day in a book about the White Nile. It is the story of the search for the source of that river, and on the opening page there was a sentence that suddenly stood out from the rest. Here it is: 'There is no record of the river ever having failed.' What a testimony to the Nile! What a testimony to Christ. 'There is no record of the river ever having failed.' How arresting the offer, how abounding the supply, how abiding the result.

Let us come back to where we started: this message is for anyone, this is for you, for me! Out of your inner being can flow continually rivers of living water. This is the ultimate objective of all that God would say to us: that in a life in which the Holy Spirit is ministering unhindered, out of that life may flow the rivers of living water. May it be so in your life and mine, for His name's sake.

22

In the garden

'Then cometh Jesus with them unto a place called Gethsemane, and saith unto the disciples, Sit ye here, while I go and pray yonder. And he took with him Peter and the two sons of Zebedee, and began to be sorrowful and very heavy. Then saith he unto them, My soul is exceeding sorrowful, even unto death; tarry ye here and watch with me. *And he went a little farther*, and fell on his face, and prayed, saying, O my Father, if it be possible, let this cup pass from me: nevertheless not as I will, but as thou wilt' (Matthew 26. 36–39).

'AND HE WENT a little farther.' And for many of us the whole course of our Christian experience will turn upon whether or not we, too, are ready to go a little farther. God's purpose for our lives and through our lives will be determined by the measure of our response, by the nature of our obedience, by the fact of our surrender, by the quality of our faith. Not that our response, or our obedience, or our surrender, or our faith are the instruments of God's blessing, but they constitute the conditioning of it. Not that they do anything in themselves, but they bring us into that relationship with God which enables Him to do in us that which is His perfect will; that which He is able to do, that which He is willing to do, that which He is waiting to do.

I want us to try to do an almost impossible thing, and that is to go together into the Garden of Gethsemane, in order that we might stand alongside our blessed Lord in the hour of His surrender to the will of the Father. I want, if I may, to suggest three simple facts that I see as I watch the Master – my Saviour, your Saviour – in the hour of His surrender to the will of the Father. And the first is this, that when Jesus Christ went a little farther he came to –

THE PLACE OF SURRENDER. I wonder whether you and I have to go a little farther than we have gone, to get to that place? As I think about the Lord kneeling there, there are two things I note about it. The first is *the quietness of the place.* The clamour of the crowd that had so often filled the ears of the Master, had died away in the distance. From the other side of the valley where a city slept, where His enemies plotted, scarcely a sound reached the garden to break the stillness. At the entrance to the garden He had left the disciples, His friends, taking with Him the three; and then He left even them, and 'He went a little farther' until He was all alone. For just a while the murmur of their voices reached Him, but gradually that murmur died away into silence until they, too, slept, and Jesus was alone.

The quietness of the place! How wrong we are when we think that spiritual crises must be marked by noise and excitement; that the place of surrender must resound to the crack of the whip as the preacher flogs the people of God. Here in the Garden of Gethsemane at the time of the greatest spiritual crisis of all time, when the Son of man, the Son of God, went a little farther until He came to the place of surrender, it was to a place of quietness, where the sound of a falling leaf might have been heard. He was alone.

May I ask very simply, have we come to that place, where every other voice has died away into silence, so that we may hear the one voice? Have we got beyond the range of the clamour of the world, that world whose standards are so strangely different from the standards of Jesus Christ? Have we got beyond the reach of the voice of our friends? So often they would seek to soften the truth, to lower the standard, to justify the wrong, to provide the excuse to condone the sin, to rationalise the conduct. And how often they, by failing to say the thing that was true, and instead by saying the thing we wanted them to say, have proved themselves unfaithful friends, although we may have thanked them for their kindness, their encouragement and their help. But is it possible that we have never found the place of true and full surrender while we were in their company? Have we yet to find that place that is so quiet that, maybe for the first time in our lives, we have really heard the will of God coming through unmistakably to us? He 'went a little farther' to get there: do we need to do the same?

It may be that our whole future is going to turn upon this very simple thing. Are we ready to go a little farther than we have ever gone before, until we come to the place of surrender? And if we do get there, we too will find that it is a quiet place!

The second thing I note concerning the place of surrender is not only the quietness of the place but the *clearness of the plan*. When our Lord found His way alone and apart, when He went that little bit farther into that unshared solitude beneath the dark shadows of the trees of the garden, He faced the will of God at a time when for Him there was no shadow of doubt as to what that will really was. Listen to the words as He prays. He talks about 'this cup', about 'thy will'. I am not concerned, and I do not think God is concerned, with that which is unknown to us, with that about which we are not clear. Surely at this time in your life and mine He is concerned with what we have come to see clearly – His will.

May I ask, have we come into that place of quietness; and as God has spoken to us just there, can we see clearly? Is the plan of God, the will of God for us, now marked by clearness? Is there something even now consciously before our minds that is God's will, something about which you have no shadow of doubt at all? We may have turned from it, we may be determined not to look at it, we may have been trying hard for days, for weeks, for months, even for years, not to see it – God's will! We have tried to hide it, we have tried to cover it up with arguments, with excuses, with reasons, with opinions; we have made up our minds that we are not going to have that old business dug up again! We have packed it down right at the back of our minds. But I want to tell you something: I believe that the God who showed us His will will dip His hands right down into that secret place in our hearts, into that corner where we have tucked the will of God away, and the hands of God are holding out to us that will right now, just as the hands of the Father held out the cup to the Son in the garden. And the place of surrender for you and for me is marked not only by the quietness of the place, but by the clearness of the plan.

So often we know perfectly well the will of God for our lives, if we have gone that little bit farther. Is there something God has told us to do, or to undo; somewhere God has told us to go, or not to go; someone God has told us to approach or to leave – it has been the will of God, it has become clear in the place of surrender. But as I look into the shadows of the Garden of Gethsemane I also get just a glimpse of –

THE PRICE OF SURRENDER. St. Luke tells us, 'Being in an agony he prayed more earnestly: and his sweat was as it were great drops of blood falling down to the ground'. Why is it that surrender to God's will is costly? I think there are two elements in our surrender to the will of God which can make it a costly thing, and the first is that so often when you and I taste the will of God we face *the word of refusal.* Listen as our Lord prays, 'Father, if it be possible, let this cup pass from me!' 'Let this cup pass, if it be possible!' Have we ever prayed a prayer like that? Have we ever prayed a prayer concerning a situation against which our whole being has cried out? Yet the doing of the will of God implies the denial of the doing of our own will. Jesus said that 'If any man will come after me, let him deny himself, and take up his cross, and follow me.' And in the Garden of Gethsemane the God–Man showed us what that could mean, for the sinless Son of God faced the will that He who was holy was to be made sin! The loving Saviour whose compassionate heart loved the world and would draw the hearts of men to Himself, faced the will that meant He was to experience the hatred of His enemies, the fickleness of the multitude, and the faithlessness of His friends. In the prime of His manhood, with His healthy body and mind in a perfection of strength which cried out for life, He faced a will that meant death. The omnipotent Son of God, whose power created the worlds, faced the will of God which meant in the eyes of man the humiliation of death and of degradation and of seeming utter defeat! There was not an element in the cross that did not revolt the heart of Christ the God–Man, apart from the will of the Father.

May I say quite simply that the doing of the will of God may mean for us this denial, this word of refusal. We may crave for fellowship and understanding, and God puts us in a lonely sphere of witness where there is not another Christian. We may plan for a prosperous and successful medical career, with its position and its comfort, and God gives us a mission hospital in India. We may crave for motherhood, with children of our own, and God sends us to Africa to care for a family of blind, unwanted girls. We may plan to get our own back on the person who wronged us, and God demands that we forgive even as we have been forgiven. We would give all that we have if only we could leave home and train for whole-time service, and God keeps us tied to a typewriter and a sink. And every time we pray, even in our agony, the prayer that Christ prayed, the prayer that is so natural to pray, 'Father, if it be possible, let this cup pass!' the word of refusal comes, 'My son, it may not pass.' The price of surrender lies in submitting to this word of refusal.

But it lies also in identifying with *the work of redemption*, for in the garden that was what the Lord was facing: the will of God meant the work of redemption on the cross. The will of God is not an abstract ethical standard, although it includes an ethical standard. The will of God is an active will, it is a redemptive will; it is action in redemption. 'The Lord is not willing that any should perish, but that *all* should come to repentance.' 'God so loved *the world* . . .' For Christ, in a unique way the work of redemption meant bearing the sins of the world on the cross; but for us, too, our surrender to God's will has as its ultimate purpose that even in our lives and through our lives that redemptive will and work will be expressed and exercised.

The price of surrender to the will of God is just this: that on you and on me God will lay the need of the world. We will find that we cannot remain inactive about the need of others, we cannot remain indifferent to the spiritual or moral or material needs of our relations, our friends, our business acquaintances, the peoples of lands overseas. If you and I come to the place of surrender to the will of God, part of the price to be paid will be found not only in submitting to the word of refusal concerning that which is natural, concerning that which is human, concerning that which I would give my all to have; but the price lies when I face the work of redemption, and realise that I cannot live selfishly, I cannot live to myself; God will take and lay upon the one that surrenders the need of the world.

That cost to Christ, in surrendering to the will of God in

the work of redemption, is beyond our knowledge; but the cost to you and to me will be none the less real. We will face it in prayer life. We will accept the burden of the sins of others, and make them our concern and the object of our prayers. The cost will demand far more time in prayer, and regular attendance at the prayer meeting. We will face it not only in our praying, we will face it in our giving. Then instead of tossing to the Lord that which we would never offer to man as a tip, we will give so that the work of God is never held up for lack of funds. We will face it in our living, whether in the demands upon our time, upon our patience, upon our homes, upon our courage, upon our very children; we will accept every demand as we seek to lead those to Christ who do not know Him. We will count no sacrifice too great to make for Him. I tell you, this business of surrendering to the will of God is not the emotion of a moment, not the singing of a hymn. It is the sacrifice of a life. It was that for Christ; and my friend, it is about time it was that for the Church of Christ. The half, more than the half – am I wrong? – of an average congregation are just playing with the will of God. Are we playing with it?

The place of surrender, and the price of surrender; and a final thought –

THE PEACE OF SURRENDER. As we look into the garden – and we scarcely dare look – as we listen, the voice of prayer finally is silent. The kneeling figure of the Master rises quietly; and that brow, damp with the sweat of His agony, turns to us again. The Master comes forth with peace in His heart and serenity on His face. He went a little farther to the place of surrender, and there in an agony of prayer He paid the price. And now He manifests the peace. His heart is not troubled any more. There are no sweat-drops like drops of blood falling to the ground now. The tenseness has gone out of His figure; peace has come. 'Then cometh he to his disciples, and saith unto them, Sleep on now, and take your

rest; behold, the hour is come when the Son of man is be-
trayed into the hands of sinners.' Then, as He catches a
glimpse of the torches, He speaks: 'Rise, let us be going;
behold, he is at hand that doth betray me.' The peace of
surrender. Have we got there yet?

What does it all mean for us when peace comes? Here
are these two simple thoughts. Peace means *the ceasing of
battle*. The coming of peace between nations means the ces-
sation of war. The nature of the struggle in the Garden of
Gethsemane is beyond our understanding, but a desperate
struggle there most surely was, to make the Son of God sweat
in an agony like that. But then, with an obedience that was
unquestioning and unreserved, the battle stopped. The voice
of prayer ceased. 'Not my will, but thine be done.' The ceasing of battle! I wonder if peace is absent from our hearts and
lives because the battle is still going on. It has been going on
for far too long! Has it been going on for years? Something
we thought we had buried deep in the past; something we
had so covered up with rationalisations, excuses, ap-
probations of friends, understatements, sympathy – we have
had the whole thing so concealed, so deep down, we thought
it had gone for good: but in all that time the battle has never
really ceased, and there has been no peace. Would it not be
wonderful if that battle stopped?

Have we entered into the peace of surrender? For I tell
you this: not only did the battle cease, but there was *the
coming of blessing*. In war, when peace comes, while something stops, something starts! In the heart and mind of Jesus
Christ, Gethsemane and the cross – separated by just a few
hours – were so close to one another that I think it would be
true to say that the stream of peace and blessing that flowed
from the cross began to flow in the garden of Gethsemane!

I wonder whether the blessing of God has ceased to flow in
your life. It has been absent for so long. Oh, I know we have
carried on with all the 'busyness' of the work of God. We
have all the vocabulary, we have all the jargon, we have all

the talk, we may even have the personality to create the 'atmosphere' that is purely human. We may have the position, but I tell you this, if you are not living the life that is surrendered to the will of God, the blessing stops. Is it true that there has not been peace in our hearts for longer than we dare to think? Is it not time that the blessing commenced again? And I will tell you where the issue was settled: it was settled in the garden, not on the cross. The battle ended there; the blessing began there!

There is an old hymn I love, but which we do not sing often. It begins like this:

> I can hear my Saviour calling,
> I can hear my Saviour calling,
> I can hear my Saviour calling;
> I'll go with Him, with Him, all the way.

And the chorus says –

> Where He leads me I will follow ...
> I'll go with Him, with Him, all the way.

And one of the verses says,

> I'll go with Him through the garden ...
> I'll go with Him, with Him, all the way.

'And he went a little farther.' Is God calling us to go a little farther than we have ever been before to the place of surrender, to pay the price of surrender, and to find the peace of surrender? Has the time come for us to tell the Lord, 'Not my will, but thine be done.' Will we tell Him? Will we too go that 'little bit farther' now?

23

Behold your king!

'Pilate saith unto them, Behold your King!' (John 19. 14).

I WANT TO bring together two verses, John 19. 5 and 14, that find their places in the same incident or series of incidents. 'Then came Jesus forth, wearing the crown of thorns, and the purple robe ... and Pilate saith unto them, Behold your King!' As I have been thinking about these verses, I have found myself held to one special purpose – namely this: that somehow or other the Holy Spirit, whose task it is to glorify Christ, might reveal to us the person of Jesus Christ who is not only Saviour but Lord. Was it Dr. Paul Rees who said once that while you cannot separate theologically the Saviourhood of Christ from His sovereignty, yet experimentally the two are too frequently and too tragically divorced. Just because we are so familiar with our need of Him in His saviourhood, it is essential that we should not fail to consider Him in His sovereignty.

Someone once said, so truly, that the secret of Christian living is the maintaining of a right relationship which is due to Him in His sovereignty. So I want to consider the aspect of the kingship, the sovereignty of Jesus Christ, as revealed in the few hours at the close of His life on earth, when we find Him named King more frequently than throughout the whole of the years of His ministry. I believe that here in essence we find all that His kingship and sovereignty implies still today.

First of all, I see here –

HIS PRESENTATION AS KING. 'Behold your King!' I find when I visit the States that our friends in America never introduce a speaker at a meeting; they *present* him. The formula they use is, 'We are so happy to present to you . . .' So here we read, 'Then came Jesus forth, wearing the crown of thorns, and the purple robe, and Pilate said, 'Behold your King!' And if contempt and cynicism tinged the colouring of his words, was there not as well an uncanny, uneasy feeling that what he was saying was but the sober truth? His presentation as King! But what happened at that moment was but the bringing into sharp and clear focus for a moment, something that had been becoming apparent ever since His birth at Bethlehem. I find in the record of the life of our Lord, *a sovereignty that men felt* when they met Him. When the Wise Men came at His birth to Bethlehem, and found the answer to their quest, 'Where is he that is born King?' to be but a babe, born in Bethlehem, we read that, 'when they were come into the house, they saw the young child with Mary his mother, and fell down, and worshipped him; and when they had opened their treasures, they presented unto him gifts; gold, and frankincense, and myrrh'. So it was at the beginning of His life; and so it proved at the end, when on the cross itself the penitent thief turned to the dying Son of God, with the prayer, 'Lord, remember me when thou comest into thy kingdom.' At the hour when the hatred of man had done its worst, and when even the disciples had forsaken Him and fled, this dying thief suddenly saw that this Christ was no criminal going to His doom, but a King marching to His throne!

In Bethlehem, at Calvary, and in between from time to time, the sovereignty of Christ seemed to break through the disguise of His humanity, and men felt it. After the feeding of the five thousand we read that Jesus perceived that they would come and take Him by force to make Him a King: as if to suggest that they had recognised something in Him that fitted Him for kingship. And on the day of His triumphal entry into Jerusalem, the anthem that the crowds chanted was, 'Blessed be the King that cometh in the name of the Lord.' And again we sense that men were aware of His sovereignty, when the mother of James and John came with the request, 'Grant that these my two sons may sit, the one on thy right hand and the other on the left, in thy kingdom' – there was this sovereignty that men felt, when they met Him. And of course, also there was *the authority that men found* when they met Him and heard Him. A King is invested with authority that exacts obedience. He rules, or He is not King. They found this authority in the words that He spoke. He taught them as one having authority. They found this authority in the works He did – 'with authority commanded he even the unclean spirits, and they obeyed'. And when that authority calmed the storm on the lake of Galilee we are told, 'they feared exceedingly, and said one to another, What manner of man is this? Even the wind and the sea obey him.'

So it was that, when Pilate brought Jesus forth wearing the crown of thorns and the purple robe, and presented Him with the words, 'Behold your King!' he was only bringing into sharp focus a truth that men were already beginning to grasp. If by some magic, some vivid miracle of the imagination or the Spirit, you could hear what they heard and see what they saw, then we should experience what they experienced – His presentation as King.

But wait a minute: that crown is a crown of thorns. That purple robe a tattered tunic. There's something more here to note. Besides His presentation as King, we have here recorded –

His Humiliation as King. For if Pilate named Him King, others would name Him thus, but only in jest or hate. *In their ignorance the soldiers named Him King.* He had been sent to them for scourging, for the carrying out of the punishment. The nature of the basic charge had somehow filtered down from the courtroom; and while the leather thongs lashed the bare back of the Son of God bound to a pillar, until the blood flowed in streams to the ground, they passed the word from mouth to mouth, 'He says he's a King!' 'The King of the Jews.' An exquisite jest.

Then as Professor Gossip suggests, 'some clever creature surpassed himself that day – a faded tunic, that would serve for royal purple; and for a sceptre, here's a reed, fit symbol for so stable a power; and now a crown – these thorns will do. And with that, the investiture was complete. And the room was all a roar of merriment. "Down on your knees, men! Don't you see the King – the King – the King!" ' They spat in His face, and they smote Him on the head, and they plucked His beard. And so He stood with the blood from the thorn wounds mingling with the spittle of ignorant fools, for whom, later, His only prayer would be, 'Father, forgive them; for they know not what they do.' But while He stands, while the taunts are flung at Him from every hand and from every corner, somehow the taunts seem to merge into truth, and the sheer sovereignty of a King breaks through the insults, the ignominy, the shame and the humiliation – the King! The King!

Then again, I find not only the ignorance of the soldiers named Him King, but in *their impenitence the scribes named Him King.* No longer in the common hall, but on the very cross they taunted Him. They scorned Him; they spurned Him. We read, 'Likewise also the chief priests and the scribes and elders mocking him said, He saved others; Himself he cannot save. If he be the King of Israel, let him now come down from the cross, and we will believe him.' And the men whose pride resented with bitter hate this man and His message that condemned them, and that threatened their position and pocket, were triumphant; but not content with the wrong, the crime to which they were parties, they must come and taunt the dying Son of God. 'The King!' they cried; 'the King of the Jews – Christ the King!' And they spat in the dust as they named Him thus!

But even as we see them have their way disposing of this disturber, as they thought, once and for all, we feel the title of scorn hardening into the title of truth. Disposed of, maybe, but not destroyed. Let me ask, Have you been in your ignorance or impenitence, humiliating thus the King? Have you been making a jest of His Lordship in your life? Have you in your impenitence said, 'Away with Him, away with Him, crucify Him'?

His presentation as King; His humiliation as King: and I see, finally –

HIS EXALTATION AS KING. We've hinted at this already; we can see *the start of His exaltation as King* right here in this rapid sequence of incidents. It started right here on the cross, 'Lord, remember me when thou comest into thy kingdom.' The dying thief could see and would worship this King marching to His throne. In minutes, the centurion is on his knees, the officer in command of the soldiers: 'When the centurion, and they that were with him, saw those things that were done, they feared greatly, saying, Truly, this was the Son of God.' In the space of a few hours, in the glory of the resurrection Mary would be at His feet, naming Him Rabboni, Master. And then Thomas would join their company with his cry of faith, 'My Lord and my God!' The start of His exaltation; a trickle that was to become a flood. And so on earth the exaltation of Christ as King, as Lord, as sovereign began. And what happened on earth was but a reflection of what was to happen so soon in heaven, where, because the Christ had humbled Himself and had become 'obedient unto death, even the death of the cross, God highly exalted him, and gave him a name which is above every name, that at the name of Jesus every knee shall bow, and every tongue confess that Jesus Christ is Lord, to the glory of God the Father'. If we can see Him here, and see here the start of His exaltation – as we look back from our standpoint now – we can see *the sweep of His exaltation*. The New Testament catches up this conception of Jesus Christ not simply as Saviour but as Lord; and Peter urges his readers, 'In your hearts reverence Christ as Lord' – and the Church of Jesus Christ all down the centuries has echoed and re-echoed the theme of the sovereignty of Jesus.

> Crown Him with many crowns,
> The Lamb upon His throne . . .

> All hail the power of Jesus' name,
> Let angels prostrate fall:
> Bring forth the royal diadem,
> And crown Him, crown Him, crown Him Lord of all . . .

> King of my life I crown Thee now;
> Thine shall the glory be;
> Lest I forget Thy thorn-crowned brow,
> Lead me to Calvary.

I think it is Dr. Leslie Weatherhead who recalls taking his saintly father-in-law to the Royal Albert Hall in London to hear Handel's Messiah. He'd never heard it before, and when the great orchestra and the great choir came to the Hallelujah Chorus, the audience rose and stood. Words and music blended into that great anthem of praise – 'He shall reign . . . King of kings and Lord of lords, forever and ever, forever and ever, Hallelujah, Hallelujah.' And Dr. Weather-head says, When we sat down I turned to my father-in-law, to find his face radiant; and the tears were trickling down his lined face.' And then his father-in-law spoke. 'It's my Saviour they're singing about,' he said. 'It's my Saviour!'

His sovereignty means that every part of my life is to be brought under His control; every moment of my life is to be lived as He shall choose. His control takes over from mine. I follow Him. I do not do what I choose, but what He says. I do not do what the crowd dictates, but what Christ desires. I crown Him, crown Him, crown Him Lord of all.

Years ago I spoke for the first time from the Keswick Convention platform, wearing a kilt. I was a scoutmaster; and in those days a testimony meeting was held at the end of the convention, and I was asked to give my testimony. A speaker at that time who made a great impression on my life, and meant so much to so many, was the Rev. W. W. Martin. How fragrant his memory, and the very sound of his voice, is to those of us who sat under his ministry. Strangely enough, I've forgotten what he said on that occasion – most of what preachers say is forgotten – but I've not forgotten the prayer with which he ended. He asked us to pray with him aloud, if we were willing, just one verse of that hymn –

> Oh, come and reign, Lord Jesus;
>   Rule over everything,
> And keep me always loyal
>   And true to Thee, my King.

Behold your King! Then came Jesus forth, wearing the crown of thorns, and the purple robe. And Pilate said unto them ... your King!

One of the choicest incidents surrounding the life of our present Queen came in her very early days. I was told this by a close friend of the royal family, so it's true. You remember how her father the king died so suddenly and tragically when she was in Africa. She seemed then to us, as a people, just a slip of a girl. And she came back to take up the crown that her father had laid down in death. Still living at that time was her grandmother, one of the most regal and splendid figures that have graced the royal family in our country,

Queen Mary. Queen Mary wrote a letter of sympathy to the new Queen Elizabeth, so young, who had to bear the weight of the crown so early. The letter was full of love and sympathy; but it's not the contents of the letter that to me seem important: it was the way the letter ended. From Queen Mary her grandmother, the regal queenly figure we had known so long, came this letter to her granddaughter, this slip of a girl now queen; and Queen Mary signed the letter, 'Your loving grandmother *and devoted subject.*' A slip of a girl? And Queen Mary was her devoted subject!

I offer you, not a slip of a girl, an earthly queen. I offer you One who was robed in purple, and who wore a crown of thorns, and was presented to His people as 'your King' – and I want to ask you, Will you make Him such? Will you take the crown and crown Him Lord of all?

All hail the power of Jesus' name.
    Let angels prostrate fall;
Bring forth the royal diadem.
    And crown Him, crown Him, crown Him, Lord of all . . .

The Lordship of Christ. 'Behold your King!'

24

Why Jesus died

'The veil of the temple was rent in twain, from the top to the bottom' (Mark 15. 38).

SOMEONE ONCE SAID that you can see a large field through a chink in the fence. There are two verses through which we can see a great deal that will help us to understand something of what lies behind the story of Christ's death upon the cross. They are Mark 15. 37–38, where we read, 'Jesus cried with a loud voice, and gave up the ghost. And the veil of the temple was rent in twain from the top to the bottom.'

The Christian Church has been divided as to what is really the symbol of our faith. There is one section of the Church that likes the crucifix: and if you were to visit that very lovely land of Austria you could hardly travel four or five miles without coming across a 'calvary' erected either by a roadside or by a bridle-path. But some of us in the Reformed tradition of the Church do not like the crucifix. Some would prefer a plain cross; although there are those who would like to do away with both! But those who prefer the simple cross feel that it speaks to us of a risen Lord. If you were to ask me which is the more correct representation I would say we really need both, because we could not have a risen Christ without a crucified one! But I want to lay aside both the crucifix and the cross as symbols of our faith, and to replace them with the very first symbol, one that was ordained by God Himself and provided by Him. The very first symbol of the significance of what Jesus Christ did for us in His death was that rent veil; that torn curtain hanging askew in the innermost sanctuary of the temple at Jerusalem. Not a crucifix, not a cross, but a curtain that was torn from top to bottom: here is a symbol that speaks vividly and clearly as to what the cross meant at least in the mind of God. I believe that this symbol, provided by God Himself, will maybe help some of us to get an insight as to what the cross was and is all about!

First of all I want you to consider what I have called –

THE PURPOSE FOR WHICH THE VEIL WAS REQUIRED. Why was the curtain or veil of the temple hanging there at all, and why was it rent from the top to the bottom at that particular moment? To discover the reason we have to trace our way back through centuries of history to the days of the wilderness wanderings of the children of Israel, to the days of the tabernacle, that portable sanctuary they carried with them wherever they went. There in the innermost sanctuary, the holy of holies, the Shekinah glory of God shone and burned. It was the symbol of the presence of their Jehovah God in their midst. And the veil was the richly coloured and embroidered curtain that veiled off that holy of holies in which were found also the Ark of the Covenant, with its golden mercy seat, and within it the tables of the law. This veil excluded men from entry into that presence. The only one allowed to enter the holy of holies was the high priest, and he only once a year, on the great day of Atonement, when he entered with blood of the sacrifice previously offered on the brazen altar outside. What, then, was the purpose for which the veil was required? What was its meaning? What was its message?

I suggest that in that veil, that curtain, as we look at it

barring the way into the innermost sanctuary where God's presence was, we can see two truths. First we see _the pride of man rebuked by God_. Did any man think he had the right to approach God? Did any man think he had the right to have fellowship with God? The veil of the temple spoke its message in unmistakable terms. 'No entry!' The road into the presence of God was blocked and barred. And the whole weight of both the Old and New Testaments underscores this truth, that it is not only difficult, it is impossible for man to approach God as he is in his own right. It doesn't matter what kind of a man he is; religious or irreligious, he cannot and will not be allowed to come into the presence of God in his own right, and have fellowship with Him. Jesus confirms this in the New Testament – 'I am the way ... no man cometh unto the Father but by me.' In the parable of the Pharisee and the publican – if it was a parable; in all probability it was an actual incident – our Lord had something very specific to say about those who 'trusted in themselves that they were righteous', and what He said was quite simply this, that they were totally unacceptable to God. The Bible goes so far as to say that even 'all our righteousnesses are as filthy rags' in the sight of Him with whom we have to do. There is a lovely but a very frightening children's hymn: we sing it, but I wonder whether we always realise what we are singing –

> There is a city bright,
> _Closed_ are its gates to sin;
> Naught that defileth,
> Naught that defileth
> Can ever enter in.

The pride of man is rebuked by that veil! God's holiness and God's righteousness are such that even our best is no use.

I remember in my father's church we had a scout troop, and a very lively scout troop it was. Many of the boys there found Christ, and the Scouts Own Bible class on a Sunday morning was often taken by the patrol leaders. I remember one boy – he was a butcher's lad, Harry Ronald – and as he was talking to the boys he was trying to bring out that even our best is not good enough for God. The illustration he used was very apt. 'You know when your mum does the washing and hangs it up on the line, it looks white until the snow comes, and then even Daz white turns grey!' Compared with the dazzling purity of a righteous and a holy God even your righteousnesses, says God – the good things about you and about me – are just like filthy rags!

This is a note that the pride and conceit of man resents today. A man who is educated, a man who may be wealthy, a man who lives a respectable life, a man who is religious and goes to church, when he is told that as far as establishing a right relationship with God is concerned, it is all of no use, doesn't like this at all. But I want to tell you that that veil of the temple had got just two words written across it: 'No entry!' I don't care who you are or what you are, and I include myself in this. You can be a minister if you like, there is no right of entry – none at all! In the veil of the temple we see the pride of man rebuked by God.

But we see also *the price of blood required by God*. The veil was not always drawn. As I have already indicated, once a year its folds were drawn back to allow one man, the high priest, to enter – although even he dared not go alone as he was. He went bearing the blood of atonement. It happened once a year on the great day of Atonement. The sins of the nation had been confessed over the heads of the two animals, the hands of the high priest had been laid upon them in identification and confession. Then the one animal was slain and with its blood the high priest entered through the veil, sprinkling the blood upon the mercy seat so that the blood came between the tables of the laws within the ark broken by man and the Shekinah glory of God shining above between the golden cherubim. 'Without the shedding of blood,' says the Scriptures, 'there is no remission of sin.' And I believe that right from the very beginning, from the time of man's first sin when animals were slain in order to provide the clothes for our first parents, the principle was laid down, taught, and made absolutely clear that sin must be punished before the sinner could be pardoned. Hence this note of necessity in what our Lord had to say about the cross. He said, 'The Son of man *must* be lifted up.' There was a divine and a human necessity about the cross. He *had* to die.

So down the centuries the veil had remained, made of blue, purple and crimson and of fine linen, with cherubims wrought thereon. It was a thing of splendour, but it shut men out from the presence of God. And it was this veil that was rent in twain from the top to the bottom. The purpose for which the veil was required speaks to us of the pride of man rebuked by God and the price of blood required by God.

Secondly, I want to note –

THE POWER WHICH THE VEIL WAS RENT. Note two wonderful things here. First, *the hand by which the veil was rent.* It was 'rent in twain from the top to the bottom'. Then it was the hand of God that did it! Not a human hand. There was a time when the climate of theological thought was hostile to the element of the miraculous or supernatural, a climate that vanished for a short while but has returned again. But in that earlier time a Professor in New College, Edinburgh, when lecturing to the students, came to this passage, and he made this comment: 'Gentlemen, here we have intermingled historic fact and poetic fancy.' Whereupon one student rose to his feet and left the room. As he reached the door the Professor halted him and said, 'Why are you leaving the room?' 'Sir,' the student replied, 'you have just kicked to pieces something I hold inexpressibly dear.' The cry of Jesus – historic fact: the rending of the veil – apparently, poetic fancy! The rending of the veil brushed aside, not because there was the least shred of evidence to justify this attitude, but just because the Professor had already made up his mind that the supernatural and the miraculous never happened! Poetic fancy! The action of God – poetic fancy! An illusion! Never! How vital it is that we should grasp the truth that on the cross God was doing something, God was in action, doing what man needed to have done for him.

When we read the story of the Passion we become conscious of the way in which so many people were involved in the crucifixion – there was the resentment of the traders in the temple, the relentless hatred of the scribes and Pharisees, the treachery of Judas, the weakness of Pilate – they all seemed to be doing things! But solidly and serenely the fact that here Christ was fulfilling the will of God comes through. As we follow the story, after seeing Him set His face steadfastly to go to Jerusalem, Jesus moves on towards the cross not as a victim but as a victor! The dying of Jesus was a doing by God; the doing of something which man could never have done for himself, but which had to be done if man was ever to be reconciled to God; a doing of something which was done once and for all, something which need never be done again!

So the silence in the temple was suddenly broken by the sound of tearing cloth. If any of the priests were there in the holy place busy about their duties, one can imagine the terror on their faces as they turned and saw this magnificent curtain just tearing apart! The hand by which the veil was rent was the hand of God, and that tells us that when Jesus was dying, God was in action. Somebody once said, 'Too many folk have a religion that is two letters short: their religion is – D O, do; where in the New Testament it is D O N E, done.'

We do well to note not only the hand by which the veil was rent, but also *the hour at which the veil was rent*. This is vital, for it is this that gives meaning and significance to it all. It was when 'Jesus cried with a loud voice, and gave up the ghost': *then* 'the veil of the temple was rent in twain from the top to the bottom'. When? When 'Jesus cried with a loud voice.' What did He cry? Just one word – 'Finished!' – or 'It is finished' as we read it in our English Bibles. The long hours of darkness had ended, in which in some mystery of suffering, the Scriptures tell us that He had borne in His body the sins of the whole world. There, as the light filtered through the clouds again, there had been that desperate cry, 'Eloi, Eloi, lama sabachthani?' – 'My God, my God, why hast thou forsaken me?' And then had come the tired whisper that had followed, 'I am so thirsty.' And then, triumphantly, what one preacher has called the greatest word ever uttered – 'Finished!' At that precise moment in the temple, in the gloom and the dark, there had come the sound of tearing cloth: 'the veil of the temple was rent in twain from the top to the bottom'.

The hand by which it was rent; the hour at which it was rent was when Jesus said 'Finished!' Can you begin to glimpse the meaning of it all? Think of the purpose for which the veil was required; think of the power by which the veil was rent. Christ's one sacrifice had been offered once and for all, for the sins of the whole world. Something fixed, something decisive, something divine has been accomplished. We bow before the mystery of it, but rejoice in the certainty of it.

Some time ago I was visiting in Armagh the home of one of my elders in my own congregation in Glasgow. I was taken into the cathedral in Armagh, and there I was shown a little statue in memory of the bishop whose wife, when in Londonderry, wrote that lovely children's hymn, 'There is a green hill far away, without a city wall'. Do you remember the verse that runs –

> We may not know, we cannot tell
> What pains He had to bear ...

There is a mystery!

> But we believe it was for us
> He hung and suffered there.
>
> He died that we might be forgiven,
> He died to make us good,
> That we might go at last to heaven,
> Saved by His precious blood.

There is certainty! Dr. Leslie Weatherhead speaks of that hymn as being for him the most profound statement on the atonement ever made – mystery and certainty – in a hymn for children! How many of us have sung that chorus –

> He did it for me, He did it for me,
> A sinner as guilty as ever could be:
> Oh, how I love Him now that I see.

This torn curtain is the divine symbol that speaks of this extraordinary, wonderful thing, that in the cross God was in action, doing for man what man could never do for himself, that man might be reconciled to God! 'Christ died for all' is the testimony of Scripture.

The purpose for which the veil was required: the power by which the veil was rent. So when I think of the hand by which it was rent, and the hour at which it was rent, I can now begin to see how the barrier that kept man out was removed, and the way was now wide open. That leads us to the final thought, and that is –

THE PERSON BY WHOM THE VEIL WAS REPLACED. The rent curtain has gone, and in its place we find the rent but risen Christ! And here we must penetrate behind the symbol to that of which the symbol speaks. In Heb. 10. 19–22 we read,

'Having therefore boldness to enter into the holiest by the blood of Jesus, by a new and living way ... through the veil, that is to say, his flesh; let us draw near ...'

Here, then, is *the entrance through which we must pass*. We come to God through Christ, and through Him alone. The Christ who is called 'the friend of sinners'; the Christ who has said, 'Him that cometh to me I will in no wise cast out': so I am assured of a welcome! The writer to the Hebrews sees so much in Christ. He is the torn and rent veil; He is the sacrifice that atones; He is the high priest who enters within the veil; He is all that God demands and He is all that man requires! So the cross which leads me to the curtain leads me to the Christ, and Christ will lead me to God! Somebody has said so truly, 'There are a thousand ways to Christ, but only one to God – through Him.' The curtain is torn, it is hanging askew and the way is open.

Here is the entrance through which we must pass: and here too is *the presence in which we may live*. As another translation puts it, 'In virtue of what the blood of Jesus has done for us, let us approach the presence of God.' This is where we were meant to live! It was the sin of a man that drove him out from that presence: it was the death of Christ that brings him back. Unworthiness there will always be, but let not a false or foolish pride or humility stitch up and rehang the temple veil! We were made for God, and through Christ and the merits of His death on the cross we can come home. 'There's a way back to God from the dark paths of sin; there's a door that is open and you may go in. At Calvary's cross is where you begin, when you come as a sinner to Jesus.' The presence in which we may live if we come.

Dr. Sangster, that wonderful Methodist whom I had the privilege of knowing and whose ministry has meant such a great deal to me, tells of an incident in his ministry at Westminster Central Hall. A drunkard came to his church and committed his life to Christ. Twenty years before he had been a church official in the Midlands, but he came to

London, took to drink and drifted to the gutter, and when he capitulated to Christ he had a pathetic hope, says Dr. Sangster, that his thirst might be quenched by some stroke of omnipotence: but it wasn't so. Often he dropped in to see Dr. Sangster and they would pray together, and one day, says the Doctor, he broke down completely and sobbed like a child. 'I know I am in the gutter,' he said, 'I know it, but oh I don't belong there, do I? Tell me I don't belong there.' And Dr. Sangster says, 'I put my arms around him and I felt a great elation even in the embarrassment of his tears. "No," I said quite positively, "you don't belong there. You belong to God. And at the last, heaven is your home." '

Not only are we to approach but we are to abide within the veil. Isn't this fantastic? That you and I walking about the streets; busy in the house; standing behind a counter; sitting behind the desk; walking down the wards; driving along the roads; you and I can live in the Presence – in the Presence! That's what we are saved for: that's what the cross is for – to bring us back and to bring us home.

We have a lovely little phrase in the language of Scotland that comes from the ordinary conversation of the ordinary folk and has also in certain circumstances deep spiritual undertones. It is a word used to describe a close and privileged degree and depth of friendship. It is derived from the times when the homes in Scotland were largely of two rooms – a but and a ben. Ian MacLaren in his book, *Beside the Bonnie Briar Bush*, tells of how the folk at Drumtochty had caught this little phrase and put it into their spiritual terminology. They were standing round the kirkyard one Sunday talking, as country folk do, of their neighbours and of one another, in a kindly way. They had mentioned this one and that one, and then somebody mentioned the name of Burnbrae (they called the folk by names of their farms and not by their proper names), and somebody said, 'What do you make of Burnbrae?' There was silence for a little while and then somebody took up this word, 'There's only one thing to be said about Burnbrae: he's far ben.' You see, in your home you had a 'but' and a 'ben': the 'but' was the ordinary room where anybody could go, but if there were those that you wanted to show peculiar honour to, you asked them into the 'ben'! It was so in human friendship. If two people were on terms of very close, privileged intimacy, you would say that they were 'far ben' with one another! Then finally the word was lifted out of the level of human and social relationships, and lifted up into the spiritual realm. When this person said 'What do you make of Burnbrae?' and somebody replied, 'There is only one thing you can say about him, and that is that he is "far ben" ' it meant 'far ben' with God – 'Far ben', through the veil, and living in the Presence!

That's what salvation is all about. It is not a kind of emotional excitement that you go through in a church service. It is coming to see that Jesus Christ has done something for you and for me that we could never have done for ourselves. That veil was blocking the way – no way through here, no entry! That was its message; and then Christ came and did something that we can't understand, and I am not surprised that we can't for when God acts, what right has man to expect to understand? Christ came and did something in His cross and passion that made it possible for sinners to come through into the presence of the Holy God and to live there. 'And Jesus cried with a loud voice, and gave up the ghost. And the veil of the temple was rent in twain from the top to the bottom.'

Do you want to know the meaning of the cross? Then if you can somehow or other close your eyes and listen with your ears, you will hear coming away back down the corridor of time the sound of tearing cloth! That's why Jesus died – so that you and I might find our way in! Isn't it wonderful? And now a holy God will company with a sinful man!

25

In the dawn light of Easter

'Night . . . morning' (John 21. 3–4).

I SUPPOSE IT would be true to say that part of the significance of Easter is that it brings a message of radiant hope to the sinful, not so much to the unbelieving sinner, but to the sinning believer. For as I read the record of those wonderful days I find my eye caught again and again by the figure of Simon Peter, the man who had denied his Lord. As I follow him through the darkness of the despair, through which so many other Christians since then have passed, even as he passed, I find the darkness giving way to the dawn of a new day of hope and of service as he meets the risen Lord by the shore of the Galilean lake. The story is told in the last chapter of St. John's Gospel. Let us begin by noting –

THE DARKNESS. In Peter's heart there was the darkness of utter despair. That is the opening theme expressed in the words 'that night'. Surely there is no night so dark as the night of some tragic failure in Christian experience. Since that moment when Peter, after his denial of his Lord, had gone out into the dark to weep bitterly, the sun had never shone again in his soul; the darkness of night had reigned. Do some of us not know something of this?

His failure was *in spite of the privileges he had known.* What privileges had been his! He had known the companionship of the Master during so many years, those years that had held for him the fullest unfolding of all that the grace and love of God had for man. All this Peter had known, and yet in spite of that he had failed. Has not Simon Peter's experience been that of others? Has it not been repeated again and again? What Christian is there but has known great privileges and yet has fallen? We have enjoyed the privilege of sitting under some outstanding ministry, we have enjoyed the fellowship of Christian friends, we have seen what God could do through our witness and service, we have seen lives changed, hearts and homes blessed. Maybe we have been blessed with all that a Christian home has meant. And yet, in spite of all these privileges, the moment of failure has come. There came the moment of sudden temptation, and disaster has overwhelmed us and with it the darkness of utter despair. We too have gone out into the night and have wept bitterly.

His failure was also *in spite of the profession he had made.* What words some of the disciples had taken up on their lips! The echo of the bold words of Simon Peter himself was still sounding in their ears, 'though all men forsake thee yet will not I'. What would our lives be if only they conformed to the language of our lips! But here again many of us find ourselves in the apostolic succession. We too have known what it is to profess so much, and with the same sincerity as Simon Peter did, and with the same result. For in spite of all we have professed, we have known what it is to give the lie to our profession and have denied the Lord we said we loved. Let us not be too quick to throw stones at Peter and his sin, unless we ourselves are guiltless of the same kind of sin; and how many of us can claim to be innocent?

How strong in such moments the pull of the old life can

become. Peter returned to Galilee with the darkness of despair in his soul, to find the tokens of his old life all around him – the nets were there, the boats were there, maybe the old companions too. All combined to call him back to the life he had lived before he had forsaken all to follow Christ. I wonder what thoughts were passing through the mind of Peter until he could stand it no longer. 'I go a-fishing,' he said. Has it not been so with many others in like case? The old life had its attractions, it seemed so much simpler. Why not try it again? The temptation has proved to be irresistible Why not try it again, and give up all this business of following Christ? Let us too go a-fishing!

But the return to the old life was not to be what Peter had expected, and we read, 'that night they caught nothing'. Poor old Peter, nothing seemed to be going right for him. He had failed at following his Lord, and now that he was back at his old way of life, failure was his lot again. He had caught 'nothing'. Do these words not describe and illustrate perfectly the experience of many who have gone back to the old ways, only to be disappointed, too! The satisfaction they had hoped to find has eluded them. There is an indescribable pathos in the words of the hymn-writer –

> What peaceful hours I once enjoyed,
>> How sweet their memory still;
> But they have left an aching void
>> The world can never fill.

But, thank God, the story of Simon does not end with the darkness, neither need the story of any Christian who has travelled that same road, for after the darkness of failure came the light of –

THE DAWN. In v. 4 we read, 'Just as day was breaking ... Jesus stood on the shore.' Some years ago a book of sermons was published with the title, *The Gospel of the Dawn*. That moment when the risen Christ appeared on the shore spelt the dawn of hope in the darkness of the despair in the heart of Simon Peter. What words are there in the whole Bible so full of poetry and beauty as these, and full as well of truth — truth that will bring the light of a new hope back into the darkened sky in our hearts and souls. For as the day dawned that morning Christ's feet stood on more than the stones of the shore, they stood on the threshold of a man's soul; and as the rays of the rising sun banished the darkness of the night from the Galilean hills and lake, so the presence of the risen Christ, Saviour of the world, banished the darkness from the heart of Peter. Thank God that even after failure, the risen Lord does not cast off the penitent soul but seeks it out, to take it and to raise it to newness of life, back into fellowship, back into service again.

In doing this we have to note two things. First, Christ brought home to Simon Peter *the realisation of his failure*. That voice that they knew so well came clearly over the water, so still in the morning light, 'Children, have you caught anything?' It has been pointed out by someone that Christ asked the very question they would not want Him to ask. Is that not His way? How many of us in our time of failure have heard the voice of God coming to us through the voice of a preacher dealing with the very thing we did not want to have dealt with. Have we not known what it has been to sit under the ministry of the Word of God dreading the moment when the speaker and the Spirit would touch and name the sin in our lives about which we were only too conscious? God cannot and does not overlook the seriousness of sin in our lives. He would seek to bring it home to our hearts and consciences until we cry out like the Psalmist, 'Day and night thy hand was heavy upon me.'

But Christ did more than bring home to Simon Peter the realisation of his failure, He brought back to the mind of Simon Peter *the remembrance of a former experience*. 'Cast the net on the right side of the ship.' At once the scene of his early days with Christ would flash back into Peter's mind, that day when he had responded so eagerly to the call of Christ, when he had so gladly left all to follow Him. Those had been the days of his first love for Christ, when there was no memory of denial and shame to darken his soul. The recollection would bring with it an almost intolerable pain. If only he could have lived over again that night in which he had denied his Lord. If only he could undo the past. But that was impossible!

How often for us also the same longing comes, when our cry is, 'Restore unto me the joy of thy salvation.' How wonderful were those early days of our Christian experience; and when the memories come tumbling back into our minds they bring with them a longing, a pain that is almost unbearable!

'When day was dawning, Jesus stood on the shore.' I wonder if the message to someone reading these words is just the same as the message was to Peter long ago. Christ had not cast him off. Christ was standing there to welcome him back into fellowship and service. And as Christ was standing there, the rays of the rising sun banished the last shadows of the night not simply from the hills but from the heart of this man. Discredited he may have been in the eyes of the world, and in the eyes of the other disciples, but Christ had searched him out to bring the dawnlight of a new day into his soul. Is that what the same Christ would do for you?

After the darkness had come the dawn, and after the dawn there came –

THE DAY. What a day that was to prove! What a glorious day, of opportunity, of service such as he had never dreamed of before, the day of Pentecost with its harvest of souls, so much else beside, a ministry that would take him all over the then known world, and the martyr's crown at its end.

As Peter moved into this new day I see him first of all *communing with his Lord*. Jesus wanted Peter alone, and so we see the two of them walking away from the rest of the disciples. We know that this is what happened because of the statement that Peter saw 'the disciple whom Jesus loved following'. How vital it is that we should get alone with our crucified yet risen Lord. I think Jesus wanted to see that was left among the ruins of the old life, and He found what He was looking for, and that was a love that was still burning amid the ashes. 'Lovest thou me?' was the question put to Peter. With a new humility that revealed the effect of the past tragedy and its lesson learned, Simon answered, 'Thou knowest all things, thou knowest that I love thee.' Three times the question was put. Was that to remind Peter of the three-fold denial of his Lord? The question was amplified with the addition of the words, 'More than these?' Was our Lord referring to the boats? Did He want to be sure that Peter was not returning for good to the old life? Or was He referring to the other disciples? We cannot be sure. But all we can see is that the old boastful arrogance was gone, and a new humility pervaded his thinking and speaking.. If Simon Peter still loved his Lord, that was enough for Jesus. And if in our hearts He finds that flame of love still burning, however feebly, it is still enough for Him. 'Lord, thou knowest all things; thou knowest that I love thee.'

I see also Peter *commissioned by his Lord*. What amazing grace is here! 'Feed my lambs ... feed my sheep.' Here surely is the amazing wonder of the mercy and grace of God, that He is prepared to take up again and use the lives that have known failure and despair. Lives that the world and the Church would discard and condemn, He is willing and ready to accept. I don't think that many congregations would have wanted Peter for their minister or pastor. I don't think that many Christian conventions would have invited Peter to come and address their meetings, not the man who had denied his Lord with oaths and curses. But Christ chose him, cleansed him, forgave him, filled him with His Spirit, and then used him mightily. And what Christ did for Peter He

has done for countless others down the centuries, others who
have travelled the same road from the darkness of despair
through the dawn-light of hope and into the glory and
splendour of a new day of usefulness and service! For them
the Christ of Easter has meant just that! Is that what the
Christ of Easter is meant to mean to you?

> Weighed down by a burden of sorrow,
> Oppressed by temptation within,
> The darkness of night overtook me,
> I wandered alone, far from Him.

> Unworthy I felt to approach Him,
> Yet longed for His friendship again.
> But how could He love one who'd grieved Him
> And caused Him such anguish and pain?

> I tried to forget Him by turning
> My eyes to the pleasures around,
> But found they were hollow and worthless,
> My soul no true happiness found.

> Too lost in my own self to notice
> The Master was there all the time,
> Following me close through the darkness
> His footsteps were planted by mine.

> I suddenly heard His soft footfall
> And looked up to see in His face
> Great longing and love and forgiveness,
> Such tenderness, infinite grace.

> Forgotten were things close behind me,
> In the light of His love they grew dim,
> Instead of the dark came the day-break
> In place of bleak nothingness – Him!

New day followed quickly the dawning,
Dispelling the gloom of the night,
My hand clasped in that of the Master
We journeyed toward the new light.

MICHAEL GREEN

Why Bother with Jesus?

By the author of You Must Be Joking *and* I Believe in the Holy Spirit.

'Why bother?' considers Michael Green, is a widespread disease among developed nations. Nothing seems to matter any more so long as we have our rise in wages, so long as the cost of beer and cigarettes is not too high, so long as we have a colour telly.

The disease has overtaken industrial life. One by one the skilled craftsmen have been dying out: the pride in work has gone. It has affected family life: politicians talk about increased standards of living, but the television has pushed out conversation, family amusements; parents find it easier to give expensive toys rather than their time and interest; the number of divorces and maladjusted children is on the increase.

The disease has taken hold of our concern for the truth. When matters of right and wrong are settled by head-count rather than principle, a moral collapse could well be in the offing.

From this grim diagnosis Michael Green asks 'Why Bother with Jesus?', looking in detail at the qualities in Jesus which make us want to learn more about him, showing how we should 'Bother because of his claims', 'Bother because he conquered death', and 'Bother because he can change your life'.

Michael Green is Rector of St Aldate's, Oxford.

J. I. PACKER
God Has Spoken

'We stand under divine judgment,' believes DR. J. I.
PACKER.

'For two generations our churches have suffered from a
famine of hearing the words of the Lord.'

'Why is this? For it is not as if the Bible were no longer read
and studied in the churches. It is read and studied a great
deal; but the trouble is that we no longer know what to make
of it . . . The result? The spiritual famine of which Amos
spoke. God judges our pride by leaving us to the barrenness,
hunger and discontent which flow from our self-induced in-
ability to hear His Word.'

J. I. PACKER
Knowing God

'The author defends and restates many of the great biblical themes . . . he illumines every doctrine he touches and commends it with courage, logic, lucidity and warmth . . . the truth he handles fires the heart. At least it fired mine, and compelled me to turn aside to worship and to pray.'

JOHN STOTT, *Church of England Newspaper*

'This book is strong meat. To read and digest it is an experience no discerning reader is likely to forget.'

Church Times

'Here is the work of an arresting, even scintillating writer, and strong argument presented with verve and imagination . . . A faithful study of this book would lead many Christians into their full inheritance.'

FRANK CUMBERS, *Methodist Recorder*